GW00730535

TRADITIONAL BEDFORDSHIRE LACE

Collar with a bold design of leaves.

Traditional Bedfordshire Lace
Technique and Patterns

BARBARA M UNDERWOOD

RUTH BEAN Carlton, Bedford

Published by
RUTH BEAN,
Victoria Farmhouse, Carlton, Bedford MK43 7LP
England

©Ruth Bean 1988
All rights reserved.
ISBN 0 903585 24 3

Photography
Miles Birch, North Bedfordshire Borough Council
Photographic Department, Cambridge University Library
Design Alan Bultitude at the September Press, Wellingborough
Typesetting Goodfellow & Egan Ltd, Cambridge
Printed in Great Britain by Jolly & Barber Ltd, Rugby

Cover: Dress Cap, p 38

To Mrs. W. M. Millar.

Contents

List of plates

Foreword

In the past little was written down and lace-making skills were passed on within families, mainly from mother to daughter, by word of mouth. With the decline of the traditional lace industry in the face of competition from machine-made lace, however, the craft itself went into decline and by the 1920s was at a low ebb. All we were left with was patterns, many unmarked, and the lace in museum collections.

Now we are in the middle of an important lace-making revival in which the craft has become an increasingly popular hobby. Lace groups have become numerous and well established, and students are looking for deeper knowledge of the history and techniques. They ask how things should be done, why this way or that, and how they can improve on what is already known. Many recognise the wealth of knowledge preserved in the traditional methods which have lain dormant for several decades, but few have ready access to the material or experienced guidance.

This need has inspired Barbara Underwood to study and record the traditional patterns and techniques, and to interpret them in her classes. I am sure that the illustrations and instructions in this book will not only consolidate any student's technique, but will also convey to a wider audience the beauty and character of our own Bedfordshire Maltese heritage.

Vi Bullard

Introduction

This book has been developed from the explanations and diagrams I have produced in class for students wanting to know what to do at particular points in a pattern. A review of the answers to these queries, collected over the years, has given me not only a comprehensive view of the commonest sticking points in working Bedfordshire lace but also guidance in the best method of explaining the solutions. The structure of the book, which is focused on points of technique and on parts of patterns, reflects this experience. I have tried to write the instructions as they were presented in class but hope that the lace-maker working a pattern at home will find this helpful and will also find here answers to the many problems that can arise.

The pieces of lace illustrated were chosen from the work of students and friends all over the country. All these lace-makers, whatever their level of proficiency, had one important thing in common — a wish to work in the same way as the original lace-makers and so to discover how they applied their skills to particular parts of a pattern. I am certain that only when these traditional methods are better understood shall we, the modern lace-makers, be able to produce lace which can truthfully be described as traditional Bedfordshire, yet still be of our own time. This book cannot therefore be the last word on traditional Bedfordshire lace, but it records our present state of knowledge and reflects a stage of development along the way.

The reader will not find a long list of written sources in this book. The knowledge it contains has been acquired largely by different methods, including talking to traditional lace-makers over a period of 25 years and studying lace in museums. An important step has been to assimilate the knowledge handed down by word of mouth and passed on by eminent early teachers like Miss Channer and Mrs Roberts. In more recent times distinguished teachers like Mrs Winifred Millar and Mrs Violet Bullard have shared their considerable knowledge with a new generation of lace-makers and I owe them both a particular debt of gratitude.

Barbara M Underwood, January 1988

Acknowledgements
I would like to thank Mrs Vi Bullard, Mrs Patricia Bury and Mrs Sandra King for reading the manuscript and for their helpful suggestions. I am grateful to my students and friends for lending their lace for inclusion in this book; to the keeper and staff at Luton Museum and the Cecil Higgins Art Gallery Bedford for kindly allowing access to the collections; to Miss Anne Buck for extensive advice and help and to Miss Andrea George, Mr Miles Birch and Mr Les Goodey for their contributions to the successful photography. Last but not least my thanks go to Mrs Bridget Cook for her work on the diagrams and to Mrs Ruth Bean for her care in all aspects of the project.

Note on Bedfordshire lace

Characteristics of design and craftsmanship. Bedfordshire lace is an East Midlands guipure lace; i.e. it has no net ground, the design being supported and connected by plaits or *brides* (Pl 1). It was derived indirectly from Italian bobbin laces, but more directly from the Maltese lace which was seen in this country at the Great Exhibition in 1851. It is one of a group of laces made in continuous lengths in the same way as Torchon, Valenciennes, Binche, and its neighbour Bucks point ground. It can be coarse enough for use as a furnishing lace, on table and bed linen, or in its finer and more intricate form, as a decoration for dress.

The lace fabric consists of continuous woven trails which form edge scallops and inner features of the design (Pl 2). Woven areas, referred to as cloth stitch or half-stitch areas, provide further features, mostly shapes of leaves and flowers (Pl 2), though other naturalistic motifs can be found in the more elaborate patterns. The surfaces of leaves and flowers are often decorated with small rectangular areas of clothwork which can be pushed up into a little knob (raised tallies) or laid flat to look like leaves, which gives the fabric an added texture and interest (Pl 3). These added decorations are worked on the upper side of the lace, the one facing the lace-maker, which in Bedfordshire lace is the 'right' side. Although nowadays these tallies or leaves are usually worked in the Maltese way, rounded with pointed ends, the traditional way was to make them straight sided with square ends and call them 'barley corns'. The whole design is held together with plaits (or *brides*, locally called 'legs') which are decorated with tiny loops or 'picots' and, at their crossings, incorporate decorative rings and circles (Pl 4).

Edgings of varying degrees of intricacy, for both dress and furnishings, have been an important feature of Bedfordshire lace. The straight edge, or 'footside', is worked on the right-hand side of the pillow and consists of a 2 or 3 pair trail plus two more pairs — edge-pair and worker pair alternating — as in most other laces of a similar type, e.g. point ground or Torchon.

The scalloped edge, or 'headside', on the left of the pattern, has on the outside a trail and a looped edging of crossed plaits decorated with picots and called a ninepin edge (Pl 5). This is because of the number of pins involved in its most common form. In the more advanced designs all, or parts of, this ninepin edge can be replaced by an edge more akin to that used in Bucks point ground laces. This is especially the case in designs with flowers and leaves (Pl 6).

The cloth stitch areas are worked as near to 90° to the footside as possible so that in a handkerchief or mat, for example, the edging will appear as an extension of the fabric centre. However, as can often be seen on pieces of lace in Museums, the very skilled workers were able to deviate from this rule in order to achieve a better flow of the design or an easier flow for the threads.

Traditional Bedfordshire lace should have *no* 'sewings', knots or turning stitches as these may give a mitred effect on the corner of a deep scallop.

The designs vary immensely and include very fine and complicated forms which can be extremely beautiful. At the other extreme are simple geometric patterns worked in very coarse thread — mostly white, and usually cotton — some of which are singularly unattractive and often made skimpily at a time when speed of making was the first priority.

Some of the finer designs, attributed to the lace dealer Thomas Lester or his mid-19th century contemporaries, still show scrolls, leaves and flowers very similar to those in their Floral Bucks point ground patterns. They can be seen in the collections of Luton Museum and the Cecil Higgins Art Gallery at Bedford and were discussed in detail by Anne Buck in *Thomas Lester, his Lace and the East Midlands Industry, 1820-1906.*

Later in the 19th century the designs contained elements taken from other laces. Honeycomb ground (see Pl 28 in Thomas Wright, *Romance of the Lace Pillow*) and Point ground fillings were taken from Bucks point, while from Honiton lace came Diamond filling to form Plaited ground, and Blossom Filling (Pl 5). Sometimes these tend to look rather out of place; Point ground does not easily fit into the centre of a Bedfordshire flower and a Honiton rose is very difficult to work in the Bedfordshire way (Pl 7). On the other hand, the designs which use Honiton fillings to form a plaited ground can be very elegant although very laborious and time-consuming to work (Pl 8).

Bedfordshire lace is a pleasing combination of geometric and floral design showing sometimes realistic flowers and leaves, and sometimes more exotic and stylised forms. Essentially the design flows; threads from a leaf or flower flow into a stem in a naturalistic way in contrast with the angular crossings of its plaited ground (Pl 8). Unlike its forebears such as Cluny and Maltese proper, Bedfordshire lace, with its characteristic flowing lines and naturalistic motifs lends itself to improvisation rather than rigid adherence to a technique. It is a lace which offers the worker scope for personal interpretation, as can be seen in the lace found in the various museum collections.

As in other types of lace-making the worker must be armed with the techniques which will not only produce reasonable reproduction of a design but also demonstrate an understanding of its characteristics.

Some similarities and differences. Maltese and Cluny laces are the ones nearest in character to the Bedfordshire Maltese lace, now simply called Bedfordshire. Interestingly enough Thomas Wright, (Romance of the Lace Pillow, Pl 29) talks about *Bucks/Maltese* in relation to this lace.

Maltese lace has the same components as Bedfordshire lace, e.g. solid trails, a plaited edge, areas of half-stitch, etc., but they are more closely arranged. It usually contains a Maltese Cross and has rounded tallies called 'wheatears' which have pointed ends. It was made in a thick cream or black silk. The strips of lace made to standard widths were often joined to make larger items such as shawls, stoles or parasols.

Cluny lace, which is usually coarse and heavy, is a white or cream French lace, so named because the designs are shown in the Cluny Museum in Paris. Worked usually with linen thread, its characteristic geometric design is very like that of the coarser Bedfordshire lace made for household and table linen. Its edging is less likely to be decorated with picots although they are often found on the plaits and are made with a single thread. Tallies have pointed ends and are rounded like those in Maltese lace. The main difference is that the trails can be divided or split because the number of pairs in them remains constant, unlike Bedfordshire lace. In Cluny, when plaits are taken into or out of a trail, they enter the trail at a sharp angle and are taken out immediately on the other side by a method of changing workers. As a result the number of pairs in the trail itself does not alter. In Bedfordshire lace, however, the plaits join and leave the trail on the same side and do not cross it, which makes for a varying number of pairs along the trail. Moreover the plaits join and leave the trail on a curve rather than at an angle.

Certain lines appearing on intricate Bedfordshire prickings could be interpreted to indicate gimps, as in Point ground lace. This is not necessarily so, and I sometimes prefer to see them as design lines enabling the lace-maker to decide how a pattern should be worked. Outlining is a feature of Point ground which has been retained in Bedfordshire lace, where it is worked in a different way. Maltese lace proper has no gimps nor has Bedfordshire Maltese. The place of the gimp in Bedfordshire lace and changes in the techniques used to work it offer scope for further research.

Using the book

In preparing this book I have assumed that the reader already has a knowledge of general lace-making techniques and a keen interest in learning more about individual laces and the way they are made. On this basis, I decided that detailed information about basic stitches and equipment was unnecessary, and besides, there are already many good books which can provide this.

As the material has evolved from students' queries on points of technique, the text, diagrams and illustrations in the book are presented as units of design together with the techniques required to work them. They are set out, as far as is practicable, in the order in which lace-makers usually tackle the various parts of a pattern, but some cross referring is unavoidable. Alternative methods of working are given where appropriate.

There are two types of Figures: general sketches, including pattern markings, and working diagrams. In some working diagrams lines represent pairs of bobbins (wd/p); in others lines represent threads to allow greater detail (wd/t). These abbreviations are also used in the captions.

The direction of work is indicated by an arrow. The crossbar of the arrow shows the 90° angle at which the worker pair should travel.

Pattern markings are also included in some diagrams. This will help the lace-maker to identify and interpret such markings on prickings or parchments.

Components of design and technique are further illustrated by pieces of finished lace. They were photographed flat and are shown in actual size with some sections enlarged 2½ times for greater detail.

Their prickings are provided in the back together with a selection of other patterns.

A number of costume accessories are shown, photographed 'in the round' to give an idea of their appearance when worn.

The chapter on reading and re-drafting of patterns is intended as a guide to those who wish to reproduce old patterns.

A glossary is provided to avoid confusion over terms, since different words describing one and the same component or point of technique have evolved in different parts of the country.

Threads

Until the 19th century all East Midlands laces were made with fine linen from Holland. Gimps were also of linen but of course thicker and more lustrous.

From the 1830s cotton began to be used. It was cheaper and easier to use, but produced looser work. Nowadays we have the same choice:

Linen is expensive and more difficult to use because it snaps easily and has the occasional slub. Linen from Belgium, 100, 120 and 140, has been used on some of the patterns in this book (140 linen is not readily available at the time of publication).

Cotton is cheaper, does not break so easily and is smoother to use but, as in the 1800s, does not give such a firm, crisp result. Many different makes of cotton are now freely available.

Although all of the threads work up differently, they can be divided roughly into 3 groups of thicknesses which can be used as equivalents. The table shows the threads, cotton or linen, suitable for each of the three types of pattern. The table is intended only as a guide since the choice of a thread is a matter of personal preference. The table also serves as a guide for the number of twists on picots.

Suggested thicknesses of thread for different types of lace

Type of pattern	Heavier	Med/Fine	Very fine
No of twists on picots	2	3	5
Linen	100	120	140
Cotton	DMC Retors 30 Tanne 30 Sylko 50	DMC Retors 50 Tanne 50 Brok 80/2	DMC Retors 60 Tanne 80 Brok 100/3
Gimp	DMC CP[1] 5 DMC FàB[2] 16	DMC CP[1] 8 DMC FàB[2] 20	DMC CP[1] 12 DMC FàB[2] 25

[1] DMC Cotton Perlé   [2] DMC Fil à Broder

TECHNIQUES

The stitches

Figure 1

Cloth stitch

Cross 2nd over 3rd.
Twist 2nd over 1st and 4th over 3rd.
Cross 2nd over 3rd (wd/t).

Figure 2

Half-stitch

Cross 2nd over 3rd.
Twist 2nd over 1st and 4th over 3rd (wd/t).

Figure 3

Cloth stitch and twist

Work a cloth stitch and then twist: 4th over 3rd and 2nd over 1st. Also called Whole stitch by some lace-makers (wd/t).

Points of technique

DIRECTION OF WORK

As already mentioned with regard to the characteristics of the lace, cloth stitch and half-stitch areas are worked at 90° to the footside edge, with a tension and texture matching as near as possible the attached fabric.

An exception to the 90° rule is the trail, in which the workers travel backwards and forwards across the passives, generally moving in a downwards direction.

WORKING CORNERS

Corners follow the same rule: the pillow is kept in position until half of the corner is worked, as shown in Fig 4a, then turned to allow the change of direction (Fig 4b).

When a design feature lies on the very corner line (Fig 4c) it may have to be worked across the corner on the bias.

As a corner may require many extra pairs, the lace-maker must be prepared to hang in as many pairs as necessary. If there is a trail the extra pairs can be incorporated into the trail and then removed. See also Removing pairs p 12.

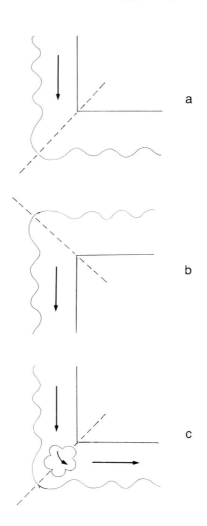

Figure 4

Turning the pillow at a corner

a-b. Dotted line shows the position at which to turn the pillow.

c. A design feature worked across the corner.

Plaits and picots

Plaits are worked with two pairs from one pin-hole to the next, making a continuous half-stitch which is pulled up tightly to a length slightly less than the distance between the pin-holes.

In Bedfordshire lace picots are normally worked with two threads. Single thread picots are rarely made and then only when very thick thread is being used.

PLAIT WITH SINGLE PICOT
Left-hand picot   Fig 5
Twist the left-hand pair three times. With the pin lift the left-hand thread, from the left; move the pin forward towards you *c*, continue round *d* and into the pin-hole *e*, leaving the thread loose. Pass the other thread round the pin clockwise *f* and then tighten both threads together. Twist twice *g*.

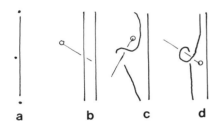

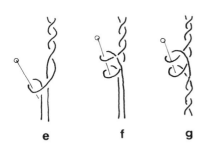

Figure 5

Working a left-hand picot

a.   Pattern marking.

b-g.   Order of working (wd/t).

Right-hand picot   Fig 6

Repeat, reading right instead of left.

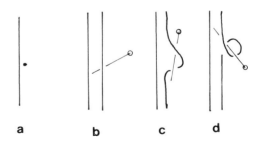

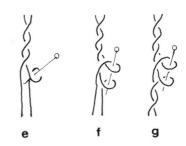

Figure 6

Working a right-hand picot

a.   Pattern marking.   b-g. Order of working (wd/t).

PLAIT WITH DOUBLE PICOTS   Fig 7
Having worked one picot make a half-stitch with the other pair before working the second picot. If the picot pin-holes are further apart or staggered work the highest one first and a cloth stitch between them.

Figure 7

Plait with double picots (wd/t)

PLAIT WITH EXTRA THREADS

Sometimes extra threads need to be carried from one part of a motif to another, as for example between stalks of flowers or leaves. These extra threads can be carried within a plait by dividing the total number of threads evenly into three or four strands and then working the plait as tightly as possible.

Some old patterns will have an extra thick marking line between repeats. This indicates that additional threads will have to be carried from one part of the design to the next (see Pl 1 and Pricking 1).

Crossings

A crossing is a point of anchorage where threads or pairs pass through each other in order to hold a section of the lace in position.

Pairs can cross in a number of ways, ranging from the simple to the more elaborate. They can be identified by their pattern markings; Figure 8 shows a pattern marking for an ordinary four pair crossing or Windmill.

Figure 8

Windmill crossing

Pattern marking.

FOUR PAIR 'QUICK WINDMILL' CROSSING   Fig 9

This four pair crossing is completed with one cloth stitch, with each pair used as one thread, and pinned in the centre: two pairs from plait *a* are crossed with two pairs from plait *b*.

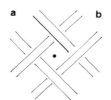

Figure 9

Windmill crossing

Four threads from plait *a* and four from plait *b* cross at a pin-hole in a cloth stitch (wd/t).

ALTERNATIVE WINDMILL CROSSING   Fig 10

This is a four pair crossing where two pairs from point *a* meet two pairs from point *b*. The crossing is worked with four cloth stitches, as follows:

Cloth stitch two centre pairs
Cloth stitch two right-hand pairs
Cloth stitch two left-hand pairs. Put up pin in the centre.
Cloth stitch two centre pairs. Pull up firmly.

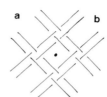

Figure 10

Alternative Windmill crossing

The threads from plaits *a* and *b* cross in four cloth stitches (wd/t).

SIX PAIR CROSSING   Fig 11

The diagram shows pattern markings for a crossing of six pairs which could be plaits or tallies. In this crossing each pair is again used as one thread. Work as follows:

Counting two threads as one,
Cross centre right pair over next pair to the right.
Put centre left pair under next pair to the left.
Cross centre right pair over left centre pair.
Move centre right pair to the right, first over and then under.
Move centre left pair to the left, first under and then over. Put up pin.
Cross centre right pair over next pair to the right.
Put centre left pair under next pair to the left.
Cross centre right pair over centre left pair.
Cross centre right pair over next pair to the right.
Put centre left pair under next pair to the left.
Pull up all pairs firmly.

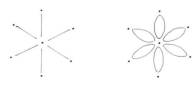

Figure 11

Six pair crossing

Pattern markings.

EIGHT PAIR CROSSING   Fig 12

Here eight pairs, either as four plaits or tallies, meet at one pin, are crossed at a pin and continue. The pairs forming the horizontal plaits or tallies will be worked either from left to right or from right to left, depending on the direction of the incoming pairs. Again using each pair as one thread, work as follows.

Work a half-stitch with each of the following four pairs: the centre pairs, the right-hand pairs, the left-hand pairs, again with the centre pairs, right-hand pairs, left-hand pairs. Put up pin.

Work a cloth stitch with the centre pairs, then with the four right-hand pairs, cross centre left over centre right. With the 4 left-hand pairs cross centre left over centre right. Pull up all pairs firmly.

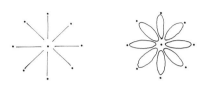

Figure 12

Eight pair crossing

Pattern markings.

HALF-STITCH BUD   Fig 13, Pls 9 & 22

Figure 13a shows the pattern markings for this type of crossing.

Follow Fig 13b and put up the top pin between the plait pairs at *a*; close with a half-stitch. Continue working in half-stitch, backwards and forwards across the bud, taking in pairs in the first half (*b* & *c*) and leaving out pairs from the second half (*d*, *e* & *f*).

Sometimes these buds have a loose and untidy appearance. This can be corrected by working two rows in the space of one, taking in and leaving out one pair at a time instead of two, and using pin-holes *b*, *c*, *d* & *e* twice. However, the bud must not be made too solid — it must not be so prominent as to detract from the main design. Also by enclosing the pins with a cloth stitch and twist instead of a half-stitch, the bud can be made to look neater.

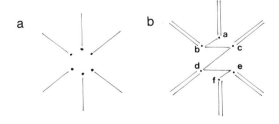

Figure 13

Half-stitch bud

a. Pattern marking.

b. Letters *a–f* show the order of working (wd/p).

THE WHEEL   Fig 14, Pl 4

This is an eight pair crossing, encircled with plaits. Extra pairs must be introduced at *x* (Fig 14b), either by hanging 4 pairs here (two pairs to work the plait to the left and two to the right), or by carrying down a double/treble plait from elsewhere to *x* — or by a combination of the two methods.

The encircling plaits are crossed with the 'spoke' plaits by windmills round to *y*, where the extra pairs must be disposed of.

Figure 14c shows a detail of pin-hole *y*.

Work a six plait crossing at *y*. Lay back one pair from both *a* and *c*; these can be cut off later. Combine the remaining pairs from *a* and *c* with the pairs at *b* to make a double (four pair) plait.

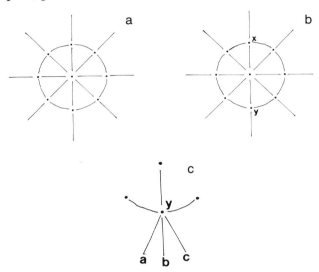

Figure 14

The wheel

a. Pattern marking.

b. Begin the wheel at *x* and finish at *y*.

c. Detail for working pin *y*. Lay back one pair each from pins *a* & *c* and amalgamate the remaining ones into a thicker plait *b* (wd/p).

The headside

In Bedfordshire lace the headside is the outer edge of the piece of lace and is worked on the left-hand side of the pattern. It is mostly scalloped and decorated with the characteristic arrangement of plaits and picots called a ninepin. The headside can also be formed by areas of cloth stitch decorated with picots (see Pl 6) or the shapes of leaves and other motifs as found on collars (see Pl 7).

Ninepin edges are made of plaits crossed with windmills and decorated with picots. There are several types. The simple ninepin edge is sometimes taken in and left out immediately, as shown in Fig 15a, and sometimes left in for one or two rows as in Fig 15b. The quick windmill crossing is usually used in this edging.

On shallow scallops the arrangements shown in Fig 15c-d can be found.

More intricate ninepin edges can be found in the finer pieces of lace. Double ninepin edges (Fig 15e-i) can be overlapping or joined with kiss stitches (see Pl 5a); others have tallies in place of some of the plaits (Fig 15f-h). In some pieces of lace the design attractively intrudes into the ninepin edge (see Pl 10) and, of course, more complex arrangements of the ninepin can be seen in deep scallops (Pl 11).

In some old laces part of the ninepin edge was worked with just one pair of twisted threads, rather than with two pairs (dotted line in Fig 15i).

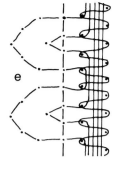

Fig e.   Double ninepin edge.

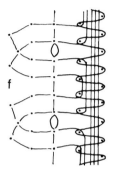

Fig f.   Overlapping ninepin edge with a tally for extra decoration.

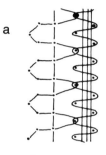

Figure 15

Ninepin edge

Fig 15a-b.   Two ways of joining the ninepin edge to the outer trail. Lines in the ninepin represent plaits; lines in the trails represent pairs.

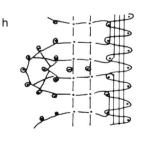

Fig g.   Double ninepin edge with extra picots.

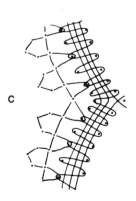
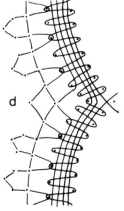

Fig c-d.   Different arrangements of the ninepin between pattern heads.

Fig h.   Example of double ninepin with the loops joined by a kiss stitch to prevent them from separating. Copied from an old piece of lace.

Fig i.   Another example of a double ninepin as found on an old piece of lace. The dotted line represents a single twisted pair.

The Footside

The footside is the straight, inner edge of a border or dress decoration and is worked on the right-hand side of the pattern. It usually consists of an edge pair alternating with a worker pair and 2 or 3 pairs of passives and is worked in cloth stitch. The workers are twisted three times round each inner edge pin, unless pairs need to be taken in or left out at the inner edge of the footside. Before and after the edge pin the workers are twisted twice while the outer edge pair is twisted three times (Fig 16a).

When the number of passives in the footside remains unchanged they and the workers can be twisted once (Fig 16b). This is called a twisted footside.

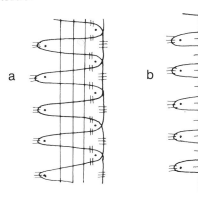

Figure 16

Forms of footside

  a. Plain footside.

  b. Twisted footside (wd/p).

Joining a plait to the footside Fig 17

Take the workers of the footside in cloth stitch through the plait pairs, twist them twice, put up pin, and continue back through the plait pairs and the footside passives, leaving out the plait pairs.

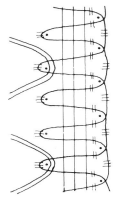

Figure 17

Joining a plait to the footside

Joining a circle or trail to the footside by a kiss stitch Fig 18

When a circle or trail runs close to the footside, a kiss stitch is often used as a connecting join. This is a type of join where the workers alone change sides, without the use of a pin. The pattern markings are shown in Figure 18a. Work as follows (Fig 18b).

Twist the workers from the footside and those from the trail, each three times; work a cloth stitch, twist again three times and continue working. The workers will have changed sides. The pin-holes are only used as position markers.

Sometimes a rectangular tally ('cucumber' tally, see p 14) is worked at this point, and will be marked on the pattern as shown in Figure 18c.

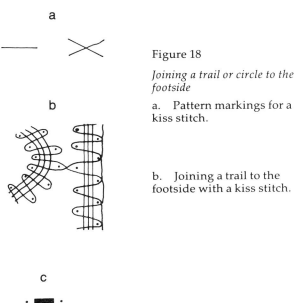

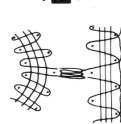

Figure 18

Joining a trail or circle to the footside

  a. Pattern markings for a kiss stitch.

  b. Joining a trail to the footside with a kiss stitch.

  c. Joining a trail to the footside with a 'cucumber' tally (wd/p).

Trails

Almost all Bedfordshire lace has a trail, usually worked in cloth stitch, occasionally in half-stitch. Raised tallies are sometimes added to the fabric of the trail for added texture (see Pl 4).

Working a trail   Fig 19a, Pl 4

The 90° to the footside rule (p 4) does not apply to the trail although it must flow in the general direction of the work (indicated by the arrow in Fig 19a) — it cannot be worked backwards.

If the trail appears to curl back on itself as illustrated in Fig 19b, then a new trail must be started at *x* and the two joined at *y*, as when joining two halves of a circle (Fig 27a, Pl 11).

Throughout the trail workers are twisted two to three times round the pin. This produces the characteristic small loops along the edges. A fairly tight texture is required to allow pairs to be taken out or added without detracting from the generally even appearance of the trail.

In a pattern with multiple trails the lace-maker must decide which trail is to be the prominent one by making one heavier and therefore more important than the other or others (Fig 19c).

If a trail accumulates too many pairs, pairs must be laid back in order to avoid a seersucker fabric effect. If, on the other hand, the trail is too thin, the eye will not be able to follow the design, so extra pairs must be added. Pairs should be added singly at the edges.

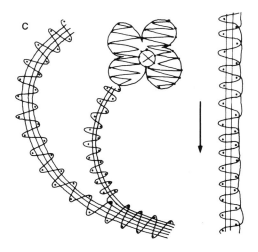

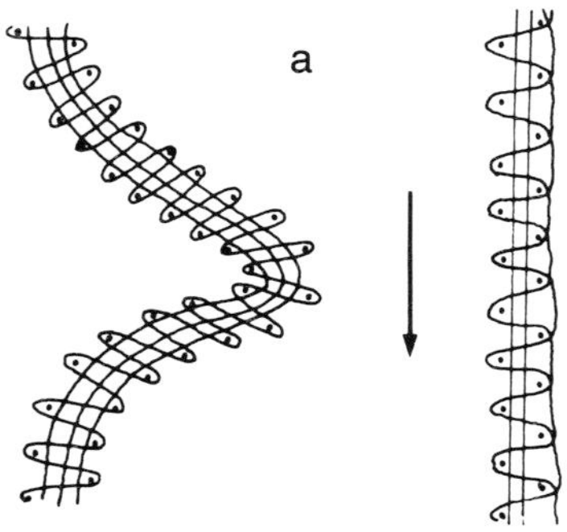

Fig 19c.   Trails of varying thicknesses are sometimes joined together (wd/p).

Joining trails   Fig 20a

Where trails join to continue as one, the workers from each trail will meet and will be worked as follows:

Twist each pair once, work a cloth stitch and twist, put up pin, work a cloth stitch, leave one of the pairs as a passive. Continue by working towards the side where the pin-hole is higher up the pattern (e.g. *x* in Fig 20a) and continue as one trail.

Often, one or both of the trails will need to be reduced before joining, to avoid bulk. To reduce, lay back two threads which have been in the trail for a good way, say ½ in (1.2 cm). Do not lay back threads lying side by side.

Dividing trails   Fig 20b

Where trails divide, work across half of the passive pairs, twist both the worker pair and the pair just worked, put up pin *x*, work a cloth stitch and twist, then take each of these two pairs as workers, one for the left and one for the right trail.

In case of an odd number of pairs in the trail you can add an extra pair here.

If there are not enough pairs to create two trails an extra pair may be added at the centre pin x to become a new pair of workers.

Sometimes a sharper division is required as shown in Fig 20c. In this case it is easier to add two pairs each, at *a* and *b*, to create a new trail consisting of three passive pairs and a worker pair.

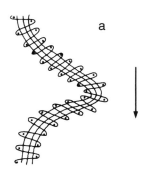

a

Figure 19

Changing direction of a trail

Fig 19a.   Example of changing direction. Arrow indicates direction of working.

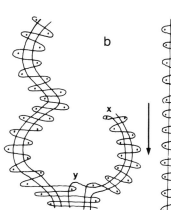

b

Fig 19b.   When the trail appears to curl back on itself, a new trail must be started at *x* and the two parts joined at *y*.

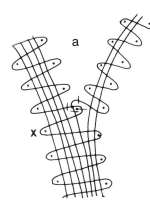

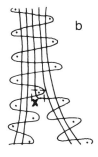

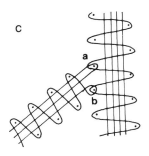

Figure 20

Joining and dividing trails

a. Joining two trails on a curve. After the join work first to the 'highest' of the next two pin-holes in the pattern; here marked *x*.

b. A trail divides into two on a curve, at pin-hole *x*.

c. Part of a trail branches off at an angle. Pairs need to be added at pin-holes *a* & *b* so as not to diminish the main trail (wd/p).

Joining a plait to a trail   Fig 21a

Work in cloth stitch across the passives and across the plait pairs. Twist the workers twice, put up pin and continue working.

If the plait pairs are likely to make the trail too bulky, lay back two threads from the row prior to taking the plait in, and another two threads in the row after the plait was taken in. Figure 21b shows the position where the threads should be taken out.

When two plaits are to be joined to a trail together, work a half-stitch with them, using two threads as one, before incorporating them into the trail.

Taking a plait from a trail   Fig 21c

Having worked the pin-hole *a* indicated for the beginning of the plait leave out the two pairs with which to make the plait.

In old laces, the two pairs were often left out separately or taken in separately at two consecutive pin-holes. Each pair would then be twisted before combining to work the plait. This is probably why on old patterns the marking for the plait lies between two pin-holes rather than clearly against one or the other.

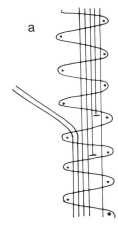

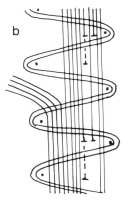

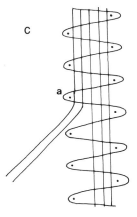

Figure 21

Joining to and taking plaits out of trails

a. Joining a plait to a trail. Note the staggered removal of excess pairs from the trail (wd/p).

b. Detail for Fig 21a. Two pairs are laid back before and two after the join. Dotted line shows how the removal of excess pairs can be staggered even further to avoid holes in the lace (wd/t).

c. Taking a plait out of a trail at *a* (wd/p).

11

Connecting trails   Fig 22, Pl 12

Trails often run close together and need to be connected without the transfer of pairs from one trail to the other. In such a case the pattern would be marked with either a straight line or crossed lines indicating a kiss stitch (see p 9), or with a solid bar indicating a cucumber tally (see p 9).

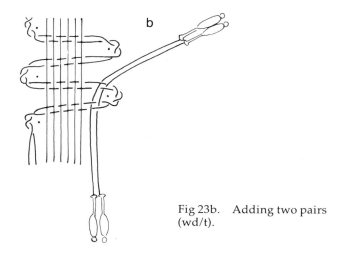

Fig 23b.   Adding two pairs (wd/t).

Figure 22

Connecting trails

Pattern markings.

Adding and removing pairs

ADDING PAIRS

At the edge of an area of clothwork Fig 23a.   Here pairs should be added singly, either in cloth stitch or in half-stitch, according to the pattern. Try to think well ahead so that pairs have been added before they are needed. Work as follows.

Hang a pair on a temporary pin x. Make the stitch with the workers and the added pair, put up edge pin, twist the workers and continue. Remember to remove the temporary pin.

When two pairs must be added at the same time an alternative method can be used (Fig 23b) which will give a less bulky result.

Lay the two pairs lengthwise across the pillow (from front to back), as shown. With the workers, work a stitch through the front pair of threads, twist the workers and put up pin, work back through the same pair of threads again and continue the clothwork, laying the threads from the back of the pillow next to their original partner.

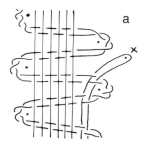

Figure 23

Adding pairs

Fig 23a.   Adding one pair at the edge of an area of clothwork, using a temporary pin *x*.

Beginning a flat or slightly curved area of clothwork Fig 23c-e.   The following technique should be used to begin a wider area of clothwork with a shallow curve or a straight edge, e.g. the flower petals in Figure 23c, requiring a length of even texture.

Begin with two pairs at the left-hand side (pin 1) and one pair on each of the other pins. Close the pin at 1. Take the right-hand pair as the workers and make a stitch with the next pair, at pin 2; twist the right-hand pair. Remove the pin at 2 and re-pin it between the two pairs. Enclose the pin. Take the right-hand pair as the workers and make a stitch with the pair at pin 3; twist the right-hand pair and re-pin at 3 between the pairs. Close the pin and take the right-hand pairs through the pair at 4 and so on.

Try not to pull the new passive pairs too tightly as this will cause them to lie too close together giving an unfortunate pinched effect.

When very fine lace is being made two pairs may be needed at each of the pin-holes *1-4* (Fig 23e), in which case they can be hung on to the pins, twisted three times and worked through as usual.

To supplement an area of clothwork Pl 2.   In the more intricate Bedfordshire patterns where there are not enough feeder pairs to create the required density of clothwork, extra pairs will be needed to create the close texture. The worker will have to decide how many pairs to add in each case. An example of this is shown in Pl 2 where nine extra pairs were required to work the solid leaf.

The gimp round an area of clothwork, e.g. in a flower with multiple petals, can be used as a means of adding pairs. See p 30 and Fig 44b.

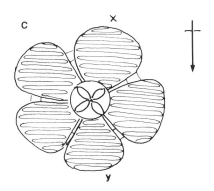

Fig 23c. Pairs will be added at *x* either singly (see Fig 23d) or doubly (see Fig 23e). At *y* pairs will be removed as illustrated in Fig 24.

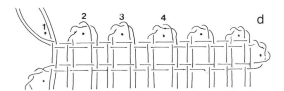

Fig 23d. Adding pairs *singly* to begin a wide area of clothwork.

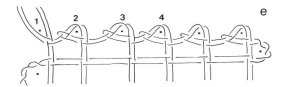

Fig 23e. Adding *two* pairs at each pin-hole to begin a wide area of clothwork (wd/t).

REMOVING PAIRS

Removing pairs from areas of cloth stitch. In an area of very tight cloth stitch, pairs may be laid to the back of the pillow and cut off at a later stage when the area is clear of pins. However, the 'pairs' laid back must not be made up of threads lying next to each other, or a hole in the lace will result. All threads laid back must first be worked in a cloth stitch and have been incorporated for some way so that they are well anchored in the fabric of the lace before being cut off.

When cutting off the laid-back threads take one at a time and run a small, sharp pair of scissors down it close to the work: snip it off very carefully.

Removing pairs from areas of half-stitch. Areas of half-stitch must be treated differently.

In the unlikely case of having to remove pairs from a half-stitch area, work towards the edge of the row; with the last but one passive pair make a cloth stitch and lay it to the back of the pillow.

Removing pairs to finish a length of clothwork Fig 23c & 24. To retain an even woven appearance over a large area of cloth stitch, with passive pairs remaining parallel to each other and in the right direction, removal of pairs in a straight line must be carried out in the following manner (Fig 24).

Start with the workers at pin-hole *1*. Twist the workers three times, put up pin, and work in cloth stitch through several pairs of passives; lay the workers back.

Take the first pair of passives (between pins *1* and *2*) and twist them three times; they are now workers. Put up pin *2* and and work in cloth stitch through several pairs of passives and lay them back.

Take the next pair of passives (between pins *2* and *3*) and twist them three times; they are now workers. Put up pin *3* and work in cloth stitch through several pairs of passives and lay them back. Continue in this way to the end of the straight edge.

Removing threads with a knot. To replace a thread which contains a knot hang one new thread from a temporary pin behind the work. Work it together with the thread with the knot for a short distance. Lay back the knotted thread and, when cleared of pins, cut off the end of both threads.

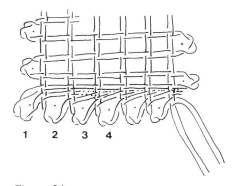

Figure 24

Removing pairs

Method of finishing a wide area of clothwork. Dotted lines show that threads can be carried on through another stitch for added firmness. The last two pairs will most likely form a plait (wd/t).

Tallies

Tallies, also called leaves, plaits or lead-work, are small blocks of lace-work, common in Bedfordshire patterns. These blocks can be square, rectangular or leaf-shaped (Fig 25a-d). They form parts of flowers, leaf sprays and grounds, as well as decorative joins between trails. Pairs are left out from a finished section to form these tallies (Fig 25a).

Tallies are made with two pairs. One of the four threads is woven over and under the other three to make a small solid block.

When the tally is shown touching the edge of the clothwork (as in Fig 25a, 1), two pairs will need to be left out to work it. When the tally is shown at a distance from the clothwork it will be made with pairs leaving the clothwork from two separate pin-holes. For a leaf-shaped tally, these pairs will be twisted according to the distance and joined together at the pin-hole found at the tip of the tally (Fig 25a, 2).

The same marking can indicate that the two pairs need to be separate in order to make a square-ended tally (Fig 25a, 3). This kind of tally, is characteristic of the earlier Bedfordshire patterns where it was called a barleycorn, while the leaf-shaped tally was called a wheatear.

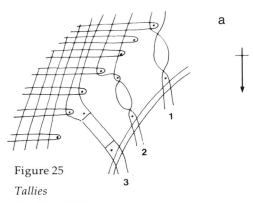

Figure 25

Tallies

Fig 25a. Different interpretations of pattern markings (wd/p).

SQUARE-ENDED TALLY   Figure 25b

Twist each pair three times, putting up the pin so that it keeps them apart. Use the second thread from the left as the weaver, and weave over and under towards the right, then back again over and under and over and so on. The shape is obtained by holding the outer threads taut and the weaver loose. When you have obtained the required length put up the next pin and twist the pairs three times. In order to retain the square-ended shape of the tally use first the pair which does *not* contain the weaver.

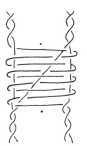

Fig 25b.   Square-ended tally.

LEAF-SHAPED TALLY   Fig 25c

Using the two pairs, work a cloth stitch and twist. Put up pin and enclose with a cloth stitch. Take the second thread from the right and use it as a weaver. Work over and under the other three threads, holding the passive threads wide apart until you reach half-way down the leaf. Then gradually bring the threads close together, all the while weaving over and under. Finish by putting up a pin and working a cloth stitch.

Fig 25c.   Leaf-shaped tally.

'CUCUMBER' TALLY   Fig 25d

This is a square-ended tally which is greater in width than in length. It is usually made as a decorative join between trails using the two pairs of workers, one from each trail (see also Connecting trails, p 12). Work as follows.

Twist each worker pair three times and put up the pins as a support. With the second thread from the left weave over and under to the right, then back again over, under and over, and so on as for a square ended tally.

Because of the shallow shape of the tally, there will be fewer rows and the weave will be loose until the workers have returned to their respective trails, one thread in each pair having changed sides in the process. The structure will be stronger if the weaver thread leaves the tally on the opposite side from the starting point. Twist the pairs three times before continuing.

14

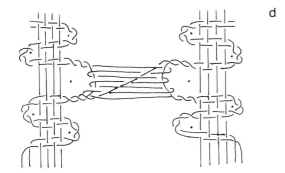

Fig 25d. 'Cucumber' tally (wd/t).

RAISED TALLY Fig 26, Pl 13

A raised tally is made within an area of clothwork or half-stitch and stands out from it. It is often found on larger areas of clothwork to vary the texture. A pin-hole surrounded by a circle indicates where a raised tally is to be made (see Fig 35b).

Method I Fig 26a. Work the clothwork area down to the level of the pin-hole and leave the workers at the side. Carefully pull all passives straight down.

If the raised tally is to be in the centre of the clothwork area, count the threads and use the centre two pairs. Put up a pin in the pin-hole between the two chosen pairs. Twist the pairs once. Make a tally with square ends, its length 1½ times its width. Place a pin crosswise under the tally to lift it up a little and prop it up behind any suitably placed pins, as shown in the diagram.

When you have completed the tally, take out the pin from behind the tally and replace it in the same pin-hole from the front, and continue working. The support pin can be removed after several rows.

When the tally pin-hole is off centre, use the pairs on either side to work it.

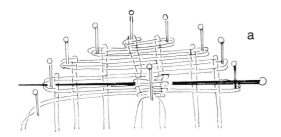

Figure 26

Raised and overlaid flat tallies

Fig 26a. Working a raised tally which can be pushed through to the under side of the lace.

This method allows the tally to be pushed through the clothwork to the other side of the lace. It is particularly useful when a pattern requires repeating in a mirror image. The lace-maker can then use the same pricking twice rather than having to re-prick, or reverse and re-mark the pattern to work the second piece.

Method II An alternative Fig 26b. Make the tally a little longer than the one described above, with the length approximately twice the width. When complete, place a support pin across the tally, on top of the two pairs. Wind the two pairs over and behind, on either side of the pin as shown. Take out the pin from behind the tally and replace it in the same pin-hole, allowing the tally to roll back. The tally will roll back over the support pin. The support pin can be taken out after several rows. The effect is a neater tally, though it cannot be pushed through to the under side of the work as in Method I.

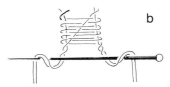

Fig 26b. Winding the pairs of a completed tally over and under a support pin which is lying *on top* of the pairs: the tally will roll back over the support pin.

However, you can obtain a tally which will roll under to the reverse side of the lace by a slight variation in the method. Follow Fig 26c.
Having completed the tally place the support pin under the two pairs and wind the threads *over* and *under* the support pin as shown; this will allow the tally to roll under itself. Great care must be taken when supporting the tally so that it can roll under the support pin and under the work.

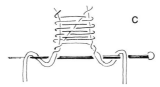

Fig 26c. Alternative. Winding the pairs of a completed tally over and under a support pin which is placed *under* the pairs: the tally will roll under the support pin and and under the work to the reverse side of the lace (wd/t).

Note. While studying the Thomas Lester collection at the Cecil Higgins Art Gallery in Bedford the author noted raised tallies not only on areas of clothwork, but also on trails, in the centre of blossom fillings, and even on windmill crossings (see Pl 4).

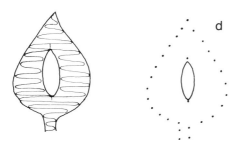

Fig 26d.   Pattern marking and sketch of a leaf with a flat overlaid tally.

OVERLAID FLAT TALLIES   Fig 26d

Although made in the same way as a raised tally, an overlaid tally, instead of being lifted or rolled, remains flat on top of the clothwork or half-stitch area. Once the tally itself is completed it is laid back in abeyance until the clothwork underneath it reaches the second pin-hole (intended for the tally). The pairs of the tally are then taken back into the work. See also Leaves with flat overlaid tallies and Pls 4 & 23.

Cloth stitch circles   Fig 27a-c, Pl 14

The cloth stitch circle and its variations is a common unit of design in Bedfordshire lace patterns. The flower design in Fig 23c is an example of this. A clothwork area separates and joins up again to form a circle, with either an open centre or a filling of crossed plaits or tallies.

Follow Figures 27a-b. Begin at the highest point of the outer circle, at *x*. There may be plaits waiting to be used, but if not hang in new pairs.

Work backwards and forwards across the top of the circle, adding pairs as necessary, until you reach the top pin-hole of the inner circle, *y*.

Work across half of the passives, plus one pair; this pair of passives should be from pin-hole *x*. Twist both pairs, put up pin, enclose pin, twist once.

Now take the left-hand pair as the worker for the left-hand side of the circle and the right-hand pair as the worker for the right-hand side of the circle. Continue each side separately, leaving out pairs to work the centre as necessary and making sure that the workers are kept at 90° to the footside (Fig 27b).

At the base of the inner circle, at *z*, join the two worker pairs as soon as the work is level. Leaving one worker pair as a passive, continue working backwards and forwards to complete the circle, leaving out pairs as the design requires, and laying back any extra pairs which were added for the circle.

Where the design shows a vertical line of circles, the extra threads may be carried from one to the next by working the connecting plaits with two threads in place of one (Fig 27c).

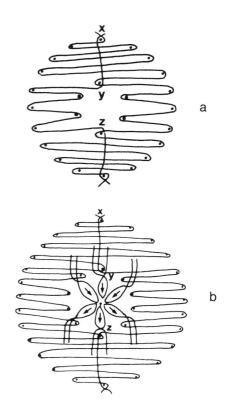

Figure 27

Cloth stitch circles

a.   Starting at *x*, the circle divides at *y* and joins again at *z*.

b.   Cloth stitch circle with a centre of crossed tallies. Arrows show how the centre is to be worked.

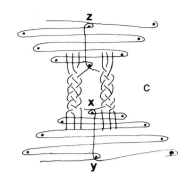

Fig 27c. Example of two circles close together. Extra pairs can be carried from one to the next in either a thicker plait or an extra plait.

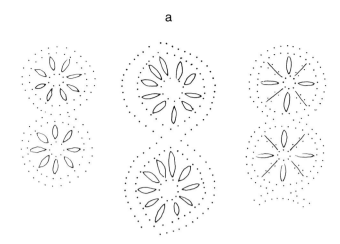

Working a line of joined circles Fig 28a-b

Although described as 'joined', the circles overlap to varying degrees as shown in Figure 28a.

Traditional method, Fig 28b. In this method, the threads remain in the same position throughout the working of the join.

After joining at *z* and changing one of the worker pairs into a passive, continue working backwards and forwards across the passives up to the top pin-hole of the next inner circle, at *y*, removing threads to avoid bulk if necessary and replacing them as required.

Continue by working the two sides of the next circle.

This method is also used for an asymmetric design. However, the results can sometimes look rather clumsy, or produce a loose, open appearance, unless extra pairs are hung in at the base of the inner circle.

Alternative method Fig 28c. Provided it does not spoil the flow of the design, the following method of crossing over the passive pairs may be used.

Having joined the two sets of workers at *z*, work back again in cloth stitch to their respective sides and leave them in abeyance at *a* and *b*. Put up pins *a* and *b*.

Work the passives from one side of the circle through the passives of the other side in cloth stitch. Pull up firmly.

Work back in cloth stitch through the passives to meet at the centre, at pin-hole *y*. Continue working the separate sides of the next circle.

When the degree of overlap between the circles results in a shallow join, a mixture of both methods can effectively be used by working the outer pairs as in the first method while crossing over the inner pairs.

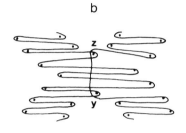

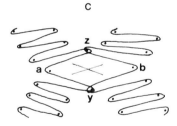

Figure 28

Joined circles

a. Examples of pattern markings.

b. Traditional method of joining circles. The first circle is joined at *z*: work continues in solid rows until the next circle divides at *y*.

c. Alternative method. The workers are joined at *z* as before; they are then worked back to their respective sides at *a* & *b* and left there in abeyance, while the passives from either side cross through each other. The workers then work through the passives and join at *y* to continue the next circle (wd/p).

Gimps   Fig 29, Pls 8 & 14

The purpose of the gimp is to highlight a motif or part of the pattern as well as an aid for adding pairs, though lace-makers have also used it to hide imperfections in their lace!

Although the finest Bedfordshire lace is of exceptional quality and now mostly in museum collections, lace made nowadays is generally of a better quality than was made in the region while the industry was in decline. Todays lace is made for pleasure rather than for a living, however, and there is more time to consider the effect to be achieved and to carry it out. Sadly, gimps were in practice often used for immediate definition where the lace was not of the best quality and in order to hide a lack of passive threads.

Examination of old lace through a magnifying glass has recently revealed that some gimps were made up of several pairs of thread from the lace fabric itself rather than of one thicker thread. Twisting and using these pairs in the same way as a gimp had the advantage that the threads could be incorporated into or taken out of the clothwork as required.

As mentioned in the Note on Bedfordshire lace, lines on an intricate Bedfordshire pricking could be taken to indicate gimps as they do in Point ground lace, but this is not necessarily so. They could equally be considered design lines, enabling the lace-maker to decide how the pattern should be worked.

Gimp threads need to be removed by overlapping underneath an area of cloth stitch. This is more difficult in Bedfordshire lace because of the open and irregular structure of the work. In Point ground, by comparison, the ground is joined to the clothwork area at regular intervals and the overlapping ends of thread can be incorporated more neatly.

Securing a gimp

A gimp thread is laid between the threads of a pair and the threads twisted before and after the gimp has been laid to hold it in position. It is also held in position by a series of nook-pin stitches. See Nook-pin below.

Gimps inside and outside pins   Fig 29a-b, Pls 12 & 14

A gimp can be laid in two different positions depending on the edge of the design motif, e.g. leaves, flowers etc. On leaves and flowers it is customary to work the gimp on the *outside* of the pins as in Point ground lace (Pl 12). The gimp is held in position by the workers, which are twisted twice both inside and outside it (Fig 29a).

When a long smooth edge is required, with few pairs having to be incorporated into or leaving the clothwork, as in Pl 14, a better effect will be achieved by laying the gimp *inside* the pins and twisting the workers very tightly round the pin to keep the gimp close to the clothwork (Fig 29b). Twist three to four times depending on the thickness of the thread.

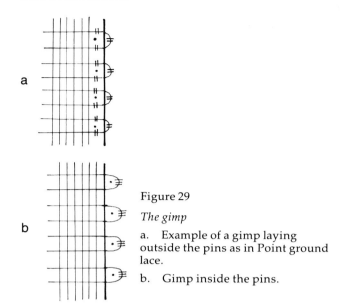

Figure 29

The gimp

a.   Example of a gimp laying outside the pins as in Point ground lace.

b.   Gimp inside the pins.

Gimps inside circles   Fig 29c-d

When a centre circle is being defined with a gimp, the gimp will lie on the inside of the pins as shown (Fig 29c). Alternatively a passive pair can be carried from pin to pin along the inside of a circle, instead of a gimp (Fig 29d), and this can be worked very attractively with a honeycomb stitch. See Grounds, p 72.

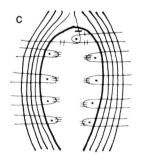

Fig 29c.   Gimp laid inside a hole.

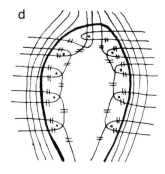

Fig 29d.   A gimp and an extra pair are carried round the inner side of a hole.

Gimps as an aid in adding pairs

Gimps can also be used to hang on extra pairs where the usual methods are difficult or impossible to work. This is particularly true for flowers with numerous tiny petals (Pl 8) where there never seem to be enough pairs for a firm texture. The technique is described in detail for the flower with multiple petals on p 30, Fig 44b.

Nook-pin

A nook-pin is a stitch used mainly to hold the gimp thread in position. Two examples are given here: at a curve between petals and at the ends of a horizontal vein.

a. At point x in Figures 30b-c the nook-pin holds the gimp at the inner curve between two petals. It is marked on patterns by a pin-hole outside the design/gimp line (Fig 30a). Work as follows.

Follow Figure 30c. Pass the gimp between the worker threads, over the right and under the left, twist the workers three times. Put up pin. Pass the gimp back through the worker threads, under the left and over the right; thus enclosing the pin as you would with two ordinary pairs. The worker will continue towards the left and the gimp towards the right.

At the nook-pin pin-holes, between the petals at the top of the flower, the worker pair will become a passive (Fig 30b & 44b-c). There should always be at least one pair of passives hanging from these points to ensure that no holes form in the clothwork. See also Flower with multiple petals, p 30.

b. When a gimp is being put round a horizontal vein of a leaf or petal a nook-pin can hold the gimp successfully at the two ends. The gimp will pass through the worker threads, the pin is put up, the workers are then twisted three times round the pin, and both continue working to their respective sides, as shown in Figure 30d.

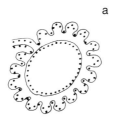

a

Figure 30

The nook-pin

a. Pattern marking showing nook-pin pin-holes outside the gimp or design line of a flower with multiple petals.

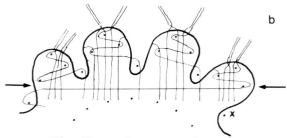

30b. The nook-pin is used between petals at the top and at the side (at *x*) to hold the gimp in position.

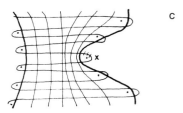

30c. Detail for pin-hole *x* in Fig 30b.

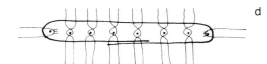

30d. The nook-pin holds the gimp in position at either end of a horizontal vein (wd/p).

Leaves

Leaves are an important feature of design in Bedfordshire lace. The representation of leaves varies from simple sprays made up of tallies (Pl 15) to solid areas of clothwork in the shape of specific leaves (Pl 16). The most common leaf motif of the solid type is the 'rose leaf'. It appears in different positions in relation to the footside, needing slightly different solutions. This in turn will determine the degree of difficulty of working. The position of the leaf in the pattern will also determine the position of the vein (or veins). This position needs special attention.

All leaves must be started at the highest point on the pattern and must be worked at an angle of 90° to the footside, with passives running as nearly as possible parallel to the footside.

Three main leaf positions will be dealt with in this section.

1. The upright leaf. This is the simplest one to work (Fig 31). The addition of a vertical vein will not complicate the working, but if side veins are included greater skills will be needed to tackle them.

Basically the leaf is worked in cloth stitch and extra pairs are added at the sides as the shape widens, to keep a firm texture. At the base of the leaf pairs must be laid back so as to keep just enough to continue the pattern. A gimp can be worked round the edge to give more definition.

19

2-3. Horizontal leaves, or leaves on a slant. Examples shown in Figure 31 have a flattened curve at the top and therefore need many extra pairs to those already in the work. As there is not enough slope for so many pairs to be added at the end of each row, the method of adding pairs given on p 12 and Fig 23d should be followed.

Veins

Leaf veins can be worked in different ways according to their angle to the footside (Fig 31) and the amount of definition required (Fig 32). Leaves come with either single or multiple veins and this too will determine the method of working.

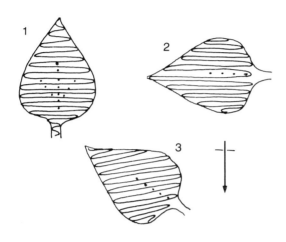

Figure 31

Main types of leaves

Leaves and veins at three main angles of work.

Leaf with a vertical vein Fig 32. Four examples of definition for a vertical vein are given.

Figure 32a. In a small leaf or flower petal with a centre vein only, twisting the workers two or three times at the centre pin-hole will give the vein adequate definition. Pins need be put up only to guide the lace-maker on the position of the vein.

Figure 32b. More definition can be achieved by dividing the leaf into two parts at the top of the vein, working the two sections separately, and then joining the workers at the centre to form the vein. To obtain the join work as follows:

Divide the passives at the first vein pin-hole as you would for a circle (p 16 Fig 27a). Work to each edge separately and back to the centre to the second pin-hole. Twist the workers twice. With the workers, make a cloth stitch and two twists, put up pin, work a cloth stitch and twist twice.

Continue in this way until the end of the vein.

A kiss stitch (Fig 32c) can be worked as an attractive alternative to a vertical vein. The centre pin-holes shown in the diagram will only be used for pins which will prop up the kiss stitch in position. See instructions on p 9.

Even greater definition can be obtained by twisting the passive pair on either side of the vein pin-holes.

Figure 32d. Another method is to insert a gimp between the passives and the vein pin-holes. To work the gimp follow instructions on p 18 and Fig 29b.

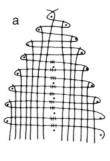

Figure 32

Outlining a vertical vein

32a. Some definition is achieved by twisting the workers at the vein pin-holes.

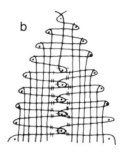

32b. More definition can be obtained by working the two halves of the leaf separately and joining the workers at the vein pin-holes in the middle.

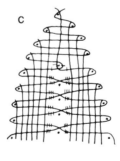

32c. This centre vein is made by working a kiss stitch.

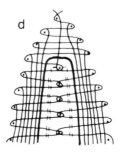

32d. Extra definition obtained by the use of a gimp round the vein (wd/p).

20

Leaf with a horizontal vein Fig 33. Four examples of a horizontal vein are given.

Figure 33a. In a small leaf a horizontal vein can be outlined by twisting each pair of *passives* twice, at the vein pin-holes. The pins will be used only to show the position of the vein.

Figure 33b. Additional definition can be obtained by twisting the workers twice between the passive pairs on the rows *before* and *after* the vein line.

Figure 33c. Still greater definition can be achieved by laying a gimp between the threads immediately before and after twisting the passive pairs.

The lace-maker should try and achieve the same degree of definition for all the veins in a leaf even when they lie at different angles although different techniques will be used for the different angles. For example, the definition for the vertical vein shown in Figure 30a matches that for Fig 31a in the horizontal position. However, the stitch shown in Fig 32b doesn't have an equivalent effect in the horizontal position. The technique given in Fig 33d matches it as closely as possible, because the vein pins are enclosed.

Figure 33d. Vein with enclosed pins. Work as follows.

Work down to the row of the vein pin-holes. Twist worker and passive pairs once, or twice (according to the amount of definition required); work a cloth stitch and twist, put up pin, enclose with a cloth stitch, and repeat the number of twists at the beginning. The left-hand pair will become a passive; the right-hand pair will become the worker for the next vein pin-hole. Repeat until the end of the vein.

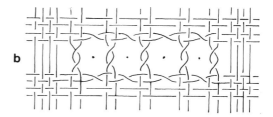

33b. More definition is obtained by twisting the workers and the passives on the rows before and after the vein pin-holes.

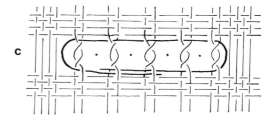

33c. Use of a gimp and twisted passives for further definition.

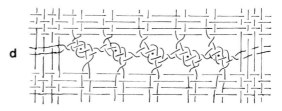

33d. Carrying an extra pair from one vein pin-hole to the next to work a stitch at each pin-hole will give added definition (wd/t).

Vein at an angle Fig 34. The vein of a small leaf lying at an angle will need special attention as each pin-hole is set on a different working row. Each pin-hole, called 'window' or 'box', is defined by having all the threads round it twisted twice and is worked as follows (Fig 34a):

Work across the passives to the vein pin-hole, twist the workers and the last pair of passives twice. Put up pin to mark position. Work a cloth stitch with the next pair and just twist the passives twice. On the return row twist the workers only, underneath the pin.

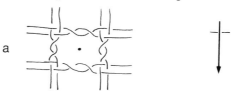

Figure 34

Working veins at an angle

a. A 'window' or 'boxed' pin-hole.

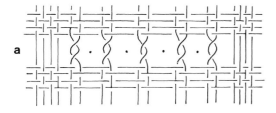

Figure 33

Outlining a horizontal vein

33a. Some definition is achieved by twisting the passives along the row of vein pin-holes.

For a complete and even vein set at an angle, follow Fig 34b and work following the direction of the arrows:

Row 1. Work across as far as pin-hole *a*. Work a cloth stitch, twist passive and workers twice, put up pin, work a cloth stitch, twist passives twice.

Row 2. Work back to pin-hole *b*. Work a cloth stitch, twist passives and workers twice, put up pin, work a cloth stitch and twist passives twice. Now twist the workers twice to complete pin-hole a before continuing.

Row 3. Work across to pin-hole *b* and twist the workers to form the base for pin-hole b; work a cloth stitch, twist the workers and passives twice, and put up pin *c*. Work a cloth stitch, twist passives only and continue.

Row 4. Work back across to pin-hole *d*. Work a cloth stitch, twist passives and workers twice, put up pin, work a cloth stitch, and twist passives twice for pin-hole *d*. Now twist workers twice to complete pin-hole c before continuing.

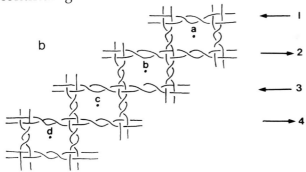

Fig 34b. Working diagonal 'boxes', one on each of four rows. The arrows indicate direction of work (wd/t).

Note. The number of boxes needed to complete a vein will depend on the thickness of the thread and hence on the number of pairs used. You may therefore need to work more boxes than the number of pin-holes marked on the pricking, so the line of boxes may become distorted. It is therefore advisable to take out the pin from each box as soon as it is completed and keep the passives pulled down firmly into position, as this will allow you to see how many boxes are needed.

Veins of larger leaves Fig 34c-d. The vein of a larger leaf needing more definition is worked in 2 separate halves, as is the leaf itself (Pl 17). The upper half of the leaf is worked first and a pair left out at each vein pin-hole. This method requires two rows of pin-holes down the vein: one for the upper half; the other for the lower half (Fig 34c).

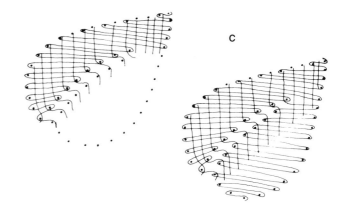

Fig 34c. A leaf and vein worked in two separate halves along two rows of pin-holes. The method gives a strong outline to the vein.

If there is not enough room to add a second row of pin-holes, work to the passive pair that was left out from the upper half, work through it and use it as the worker for the next row (Fig 34d).

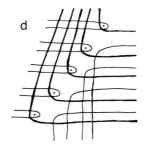

Fig 34d. Working a leaf and vein in two halves when there is no room for a second row of pin-holes at the vein line. Passives from the first half become workers for the second half as shown by the thicker lines (wd/p).

Side veins

Side veins add to the complexity of leaves with a central vein (Fig 35a). They can be worked in the same way as the centre vein, but a method giving less definition should be used, and each vein treated according to its angle.

Leaves with raised tallies

Leaves often have raised tallies for decoration instead of side veins (Fig 35b). They are worked as ordinary raised tallies. See Pl 16 & Fig 26b.

Leaves decorated with flat overlaid tallies Pl 4

In some patterns the tallies, instead of being raised, are laid down flat over the clothwork area as a surface decoration (Pl 4). In older patterns this surface decoration would be laid over areas of cloth stitch whereas more recently workers have tended to use a background of half-stitch. Like the raised tallies, the overlaid flat tallies are worked on top of the clothwork — the 'right side' of the lace.

More added pairs will be required to work a leaf in cloth stitch than in half-stitch, but they can be easily removed by being laid back at the bottom of the leaf.

It is more difficult to remove extra pairs at the bottom of a leaf worked in half-stitch, but since it can be worked with fewer pairs anyway, the problem is reduced. If it is essential to remove pairs from the half-stitch, make sure that the removed pair is near to an edge and has been worked in a cloth stitch first. See Removing pairs p 13.

As the width of underlying leaves varies, two methods for working overlaid tallies are given. The first is more suitable for narrow leaves, the second for more bulbous ones where the width will require more pairs to work it.

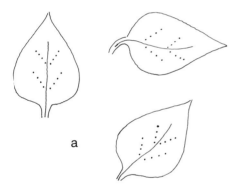

Figure 35

Leaves with side veins or raised tallies

35a.   Positions of side veins.

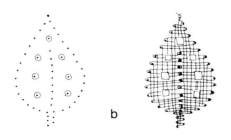

35b.   Pattern marking and work outline for raised tallies used instead of side veins.

Flat overlaid tallies on narrow leaves Figs 36a-b.   Figure 36a shows pattern markings for this type of leaf and Fig 36b illustrates the stages of working.

The leaf will be completed in five stages, with the overlaid tallies unit *c,d,e* being laid to the back of the pillow while the clothwork underneath it is brought level with *e*. By this method the lace-maker uses only the pairs already available.

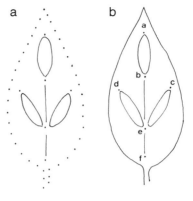

Figure 36

Flat overlaid tallies

a.   Pattern marking.

b.   Order of working the tallies; Methods I & II.

Work the leaf itself down to the level at *a*. Put up a pin at *a* and, with the pairs on either side, work a pointed-end tally long enough to reach pin-hole *b*. Lay it to the back and work the clothwork area until it is level with pin-hole *b*. Bring the leaf forward and put up pin *b* between the two leaf pairs, having arranged all the other passives evenly across the work. Work one row across the leaf. Take the two pairs nearest to pin *b* and work a plait long enough to reach pin-hole *e*. Lay it to the back of the pillow.

Work the clothwork area until it is level with pin-hole *c* and/or *d*. Leave the workers at the edge and pull the passives into position. Put up pin at *c* and, with the pairs from either side, work a pointed-end tally long enough to reach *e*. Bring forward the plait from *b* and work a windmill at *e*.

Work another tally long enough to reach pin-hole *d*. Put up pin at *d* between the tally pairs, making sure that it is correctly placed in relation to the other passives. Take the two pairs into the next row of work. Take out pin *e* and lay to the back the unit containing the two tallies and the stalk plait. Continue working the clothwork area until it has reached the level of pin-hole *e*. Bring the leaf unit forward into position, put up pin between the two pairs and work one row across.

Take the pairs nearest to the pin to make a plait long enough to reach pin-hole *f*. Lay the plait to the back of the pillow until the cloth-work area is level with pin-hole *f* and then bring the pairs back into the work.

Overlaid tallies on wider leaves Fig 36c, Pl 23. This method is suitable for working a more

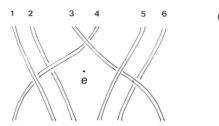

36c. Detail for pin-hole *e* in Method II. Each of the six pairs is treated as one thread (wd/t).

bulbous leaf shape because there will be extra pairs in the work. It is considered by some as the traditional way of working overlaid tallies.

Follow the directions for the first method to pin-hole *b*, adding extra pairs if necessary. Make a tally with the passives at both *c* and *d* long enough to reach to *e*. Lay them back until the work is level with *e*, leaving the worker at the side, out of the way. Bring the tallies and 'stalk' forward. There will now be six pairs here. Using each pair as one thread, work a crossing at pin-hole *e*, following Figure 36c.

Cross pair 3: over 4, under 5 and over 6. Cross pair 4: over 2 and under 1. Put up pin *e*.

The six pairs are now the centre passives for the underlying leaf. Continue working, leaving out the centre two pairs to complete the stalk.

Leaves with holes Fig 37, Pl 18
Instead of a vein, a hole or a cluster of holes is sometimes left in the clothwork area of the leaf, for decoration. An example of this can be seen in Pl 18, where the holes in the clothwork make up the shape of a small composite leaf. Simple round holes are worked in the same way as the inner part of a circle. See Circles p 16 and Fig 37a.

A cluster of holes Fig 37b. As can be seen from the example in Figure 37b, filling the gaps between the holes set at different angles will require extra care. You may find there are no passives where you want them, but several where you don't! Many pairs have to be added at the base of a hole to complete it, merely to be carried through the nar-row area of clothwork to the next hole where they will need to be removed. It is more practical to lay a gimp inside each hole; it will give the design a

greater definition as well as filling some of the small holes which inevitably appear in the clothwork. The disadvantage of a gimp in this case is that the thread ends must be crossed at the base of each hole and this tends to give the lace a bulky appearance, especially in the narrow areas between the holes.

The individual lace-maker must decide whether to accept this bulky effect, or to cross the ends through the clothwork and carry on to the next hole.

As an alternative to a gimp you may find it easier to use one of the following: a passive pair, as an 'outliner' on the inside of the circle pins (Fig 37c); an edge pair, see Footside p 9; an edge pair worked with a honeycomb stitch, see Grounds p 72.

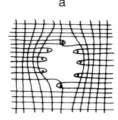

Figure 37

Leaves with holes

a. A hole in the clothwork worked like the inside of a circle.

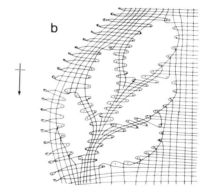

37b. Holes in the cloth work forming a composite leaf.

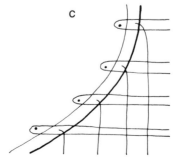

37c. An extra pair is carried round the inside of the hole for added neatness (wd/p).

Oak leaves   Fig 38a–e, Pl 19

An example of this motif can be seen on Pl 19. The leaves are worked in cloth stitch with veins of equal definition. Leaves may have a gimp round the outside, but always have a continuous gimp round the veins (Fig 38a). The veins are wide and open and keeping their appearance neat can be difficult as the vein joints tend to be loose. A tidier effect can be achieved if an extra pair is included at each vein pin-hole (making three pairs at a pin-hole) and carried over to the following pin-hole, as shown in Figure 38b. The areas of cloth stitch between the veins are best worked in blocks, one at a time.

Blocking Fig 38c.   A leaf set at an angle can be worked quite successfully in sections or blocks, in the order suggested by the numbers. I have used the term 'blocking' to describe this method which can be applied to areas of clothwork between veins of leaves or other motifs set at any angle.

Begin the clothwork at the two highest points *a* & *b*, joining the workers of the two sides at w. When you get to the tip of the vein at *x* & *y* continue working only the centre passives to complete block 1 at pin-hole *z*, leaving the side passives in abeyance and leaving out a pair of passives at each vein pin-hole until you reach pin-hole *z*.

Return to pin *x*. Take the passive pair left out at *x* as a worker pair (Fig 38d). Work to the right edge and back, and then work through the passive pair left out at the second vein pin-hole. Leave the worker pair here as a passive and use the pair which was left out at the second vein pin-hole as a worker. Work to the right and back and continue, as shown in the diagram (Fig 38d) to finish block 2.

Work blocks 3, 4 & 5 in the same way.

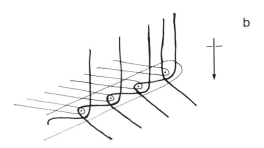

38b.   An extra pair is included at each vein pin-hole to prevent the vein from spreading out (wd/t).

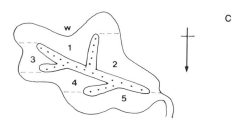

38c.   Dividing a leaf into 'blocks' for ease of working.

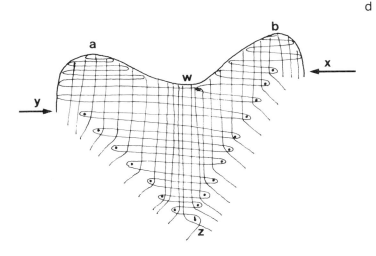

38d.   Detail for working block 1. Starting separately at *a* & *b* the workers join at *w*. Work divides again at the tip of the two veins at *x* and *y* and the block is completed at *z*. Pairs are left out at each vein pin-hole all the way down to *z* (wd/p).

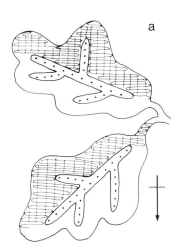

Figure 38

Oak leaves and acorns

a.   Two leaves at different angles with wide veining. The first half in each leaf is worked at the appropriate angle. A continuous gimp is laid all the way round the veining.

e

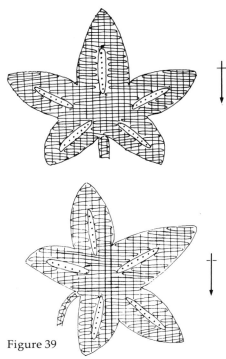

38e. Starting block 2. Work starts at the tip of the upright vein, at *x*. Passive pairs left out at the vein pin-holes in block 1 become workers and then passives again in block 2. For example, the passive pair left out at pin-hole *x* becomes the worker for block 2, works through the passives to the edge of the leaf, returns to the next vein pin-hole, where it works a stitch with the passive left out at that pin-hole and becomes a passive pair as shown (wd/p).

Figure 39

Ivy leaves

Two leaves at different angles in relation to the direction of work (see arrows). In both examples each vein has a gimp round it, though there are no gimps on the outside edge of the leaf.

Flowers

Flower motifs abound in Bedfordshire lace and come in many forms, from the simplest made up of tallies (Pl 6) to the more complex (Pl 24) and naturalistic ones adapted from Honiton lace (Pl 7). The majority, however, are composed of four or more solid-area petals (Fig 40a) which are worked in the same manner as leaves.

Flower with a centre of crossed tallies   Fig 40a-f

This flower has five solid petals with four crossed tallies in the centre. Work as follows:

Begin work at the top pin-hole of petal 1.

If there are not enough pairs to create a firm texture, add pairs as you would for a leaf (see p 12).

If a gimp is required, for extra definition, it must be placed between the pairs that begin the petal. As the petal widens pairs must be added to give a uniform texture to the flower. As the width of the petal decreases towards its base, pairs should be left out at the sides to be incorporated into the side petals.

Work (as for a Circle, p 16) to the top pin-hole of the inner circle, put up pin, enclose the pin, twist the pairs and use these two pairs as workers to complete either side of petal 1.

Acorns   Fig 38f, Pl 19

Acorns are usually worked in two stitches: the nut in whole stitch and the cup in half-stitch. Gimps are worked first round one section, crossed between the two parts to continue round the other part in a figure of eight.

When pin-holes between the nut and cup are horizontal they are used just as holding pins, to prop the gimps into position. An extra pin-hole, *x*, is sometimes found on either side of the dividing line. It is worked as a nook-pin (see, p 19) to hold the gimp in position and to help establish the rounded shape of the cup.

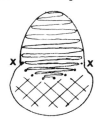

f

Fig 38f. Acorn. The nut is normally worked in cloth stitch and the cup in half-stitch. In some patterns nook-pins are worked at *x* to hold the gimp in position.

Ivy leaves   Fig 39, Pl 10

Plate 10 shows an arrangement of veined ivy leaves. The leaf is always worked in cloth stitch. It very rarely has a gimp on the outside but always one enclosing the five veins (Fig 39). As these leaves lie at many different angles each has to be tackled individually and to be worked in blocks like the oak leaves (see above).

Several parts of an ivy leaf require particular attention:
a. The centre will need extra pairs to fill in gaps left by the veins. These are best hung on the gimps at the bottom of vertical or near-vertical veins.
b. Sufficient extra pairs must be allowed to work the centre in order to keep it solid.
c. In order to obtain the correct shape for the pointed leaves pairs must be added and removed. See pp 12–13 and Figs 23d & 24.

A gimp for the inner circle can be added at this top pin-hole.

Complete each side of petal *1* separately, leaving out two pairs in the correct position for the centre tallies.

When petal *1* is completed two or three pairs may be carried as passives round the edge of the centre circle (*x* in Fig 40d-f) instead of, or as well as, a gimp to keep the shape firm.

Start petals *2* and *3* at the top. Work in cloth stitch, taking in pairs that were left out from petal *1*, adding pairs where necessary. Work until the lower edges of petals *2* and *3* (Fig 40d-e).

The lower edges of these petals could be horizontal (Fig 40d) or continue below point *y* as in Figure 40e. When the base of petal *2* is level with point *y* put up pins between the passive pairs and plait the passive pairs to the pin-holes of petal *4* (Fig 40d). Put up pins as props between the pairs. With the worker work back from the centre pin-hole *y* to begin petal *4*.

When the base of petal *2* (and the top of petal *4*) is at an angle to pin-hole *y* (Fig 40e), continue working the petal, leaving out pairs at each pin-hole to be taken into petal *4*, as shown. Begin petal *4* at *z* with a new worker and work petal *4*, taking in the pairs left out from petal *3*.

Return to the centre tallies. Having worked the two upper tallies, cross them with a windmill in the centre and work the two lower ones. Threads from these tallies must be incorporated into the petals at the appropriate position to match the upper half.

Work petal *4* and *5* down to point *t* on the inner circle where they will join (Fig 40f). Bring both pairs of workers to the centre pin-hole *t*.

In order to prevent holes forming in the fabric, it is sometimes necessary to hang on extra pairs at the base of the inner circle, on either side of pin-hole *t*, before separating them to continue working petals *4* and *5*.

Work a row or two across both petals *4* and *5* before dividing them as shown in Figure 40f.

Work down both petals simultaneously, so that they can be joined, either by leaving out a pair to cross to the other petal (and back again), or by working a kiss stitch. These joining stitches should match up as far as possible the joins between the other petals. After this, either petal can be finished separately, taking out pairs to leave the correct number for finishing (see Removing pairs, p 13).

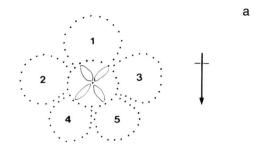

Figure 40

Flower with or without a centre

a.   Pattern marking. Numbers show order of working the solid petals.

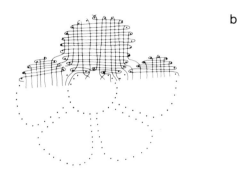

40b.   Working petal 1 and parts of petals 2 & 3. Work divides into two halves at the top pin-hole of the inner circle and then continues as for a basic circle.

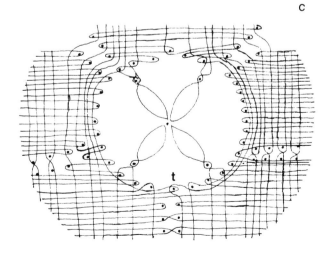

40c.   Having worked both halves round, and the tallies in the centre, the circle is joined at the bottom (wd/p).

27

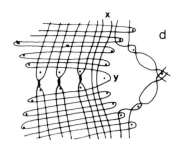

Fig 40d. Horizontal division between petals. Passive pairs are plaited together to form the join. Several passives, *x*, can be carried round the inner circle (wd/p).

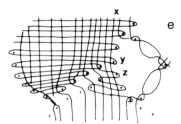

Fig 40e. Diagonal division between petals. The upper petal is completed first. Pairs are left out at each pin-hole and are incorporated into the lower petal. The lower petal starts at *z* with a new worker (wd/p).

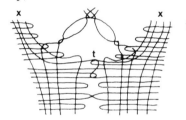

Fig 40f. Vertical division between two lower petals. Pairs must join in places to match the other joins in the flower, either in a kiss stitch or with a single twisted pair travelling backwards and forwards between the two petals (wd/p).

Flower with raised tallies on petals Fig 41a, Pl 15

This resembles the flower shown in Fig 40, but has a raised tally on each petal.

Work the cloth stitch area down to the level of the pin-hole and mark the beginning of the tally. Leave the workers at the edge and pull the passives into position. Put up the pin, and take a pair of passives from either side of the pin to work a square-ended tally, with the length 1½ times its width. See Tallies, p 14). Continue as for Flower with a centre of crossed tallies (Fig 40).

Flower with centre veins on petals Fig 41b, Pl 16

This too resembles the flower in Figure 40 except that it has a centre vein on the petals.

As petal *1* is usually vertical, you can work the vein by twisting the workers at the pin-holes as shown; put up the pin, merely to show the position of the twists and to 'prop up' the work.

To give more definition to the vein also twist the passive pair on either side of the pin.

Petals *2* and *3* are usually horizontal. This allows the vein to be made by twisting the passives at the pin-holes shown.

For further definition twist the workers on the rows *before* and *after* the one where the passives are twisted, just as for the leaf vein in Figure 33a.

Petals *4* and *5* are usually at an angle so the 'boxes' method, in which the pairs are twisted all round the pin-hole, must be used. See Leaf with a vein at an angle, p 21, Fig 34.

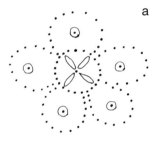

Figure 41

Flowers with decorated petals

a. Pattern markings for raised tallies.

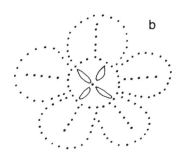

41b. Pattern markings for veins.

28

Flower with a half-stitch centre   Fig 42, Pl 20

This type of flower is worked in the same way as the previous ones, except for its half-stitch centre which needs special attention. The centre is usually decorated with one or more raised tallies.

First work petal *1* down to *a*, the top pin-hole of the centre circle, then petals *2* and *3* to the same level, as shown (Fig 42a).

After enclosing pin-hole *a* use the two pairs of workers to complete petal *1* on either side, until pin-holes *b* & *c*.

Depending on the thickness of thread, two to four pairs of passives will be left out at pin-hole *a* ready to begin the half-stitch centre. As the left-hand side petal workers return to pin-hole *b* additional passive pairs from petal *1* will be left out to work the half-stitch centre.

Now work a half-stitch from pin-hole *a* to pin-hole *b*; the two pairs of workers meeting and enclosing pin *b*. With the left-hand worker from pin *b* continue to the left in cloth stitch as in previous flowers.

With the right-hand pair of workers work to the right in half-stitch to pin-hole *c*, taking in two more pairs of passives from petal *1* and meeting the workers from the right-hand side of the petal. Put up pin *c* and enclose it.

With the right-hand pairs of workers from pin *c* work to the right in cloth stitch, leaving out passive pairs to work the centre. With the left-hand pair of workers from pin *c* work to the left in half-stitch to the next pin-hole on the inner circle.

Continue working the flower across all three parts simultaneously, keeping petals and centre level. Join the workers from the cloth stitch petals, with the workers from the centre half-stitch, at the inner ring of pin-holes. Take the passives from the petals into the centre (instead of laying them back), as necessary, to obtain an even texture. After working half-way down the flower leave out pairs from the centre to work petals *4* & *5* matching the top half of the flower (see Fig 42b).

When a raised tally is marked on the pricking, pull the passives into position, put up pin and make the raised tally with the pairs on either side of the pin. See Raised tallies, p 15).

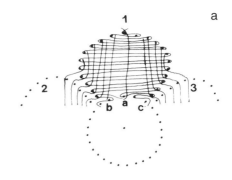

Figure 42

Flower with a half-stitch centre

a.   Beginning the flower. At pin-hole *a* the work separates. At pin-holes *b* & *c* passive pairs will be left out to work the half-stitch centre (wd/p).

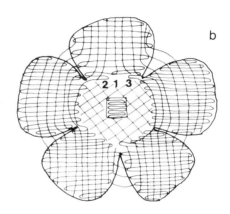

42b.   Sketch showing the angle of work of the completed flower.

Rose flowers   Fig 43, Pls 3 & 21

This interpretation of a rose is illustrated in Pls 3 & 21. Sometimes the centre of the flower is made of a crossing of tallies as in Figure 43a, and sometimes in Point ground as in Figure 43b. The two versions are worked differently because of their centre fillings. The two sides of the flower in Figure 43a can be worked separately, while both sides of Flower 43b will be worked simultaneously, in step with the progress of the Point ground centre.

Rose with a centre of crossed tallies   Fig 43a

Work the petals in the order shown. This order allows pairs from petal 3, left out at each pin-hole, to be fed into petal 4, and into half of petal 5, as shown by the arrows. These pairs will be left out again from the second half of petal 5 and petal 6 to work petal 7.

Leave out pairs from petals 2 and 4 as shown to work three tallies. They will also work a half-stitch bud centre and three more tallies to match the upper three, completing the centre and feeding into petals 5, 6 & 9. Petal 8 should have been completed earlier.

Petals 7 & 9 can be completed, leaving out pairs to work petal 10 and re-using the pin-holes between the petals or changing workers. See Blocking, p 25.

Alternatively, petals 7, 9 & 10 can be finished together, with their three sets of workers meeting at the join pin-holes and continuing to work their own section.

a

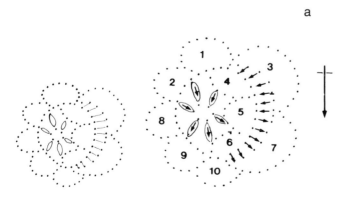

Figure 43

Rose flowers

a. Pattern marking for a rose with a centre of tallies, and order of working the petals. Arrows show where pairs are fed into other parts of the flower.

Rose with a Point ground centre Fig 43b and Pl 21. Because of the Point ground centre both sides must be worked almost simultaneously, with the left-hand side slightly ahead to allow for the angle of the ground.

Remember that every row of the Point ground must be worked completely so that it is joined into the clothwork at both ends, as in Floral Bucks Point ground.

Gimps may be incorporated to highlight a design feature in either flower, for example: around petals 4, 5 & 6 in Figure 43a, or around the centre ground in Figure 43b.

If all four right-hand petals of the flower in Fig 43b were gimped they would stand out prominently, giving an added dimension to the design.

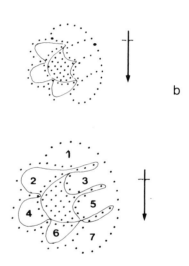

b

43b.   Pattern marking for a rose with a Point ground centre, and order of working the petals.

Flower with multiple petals   Fig 44, Pl 8

The edging in Pl 8 contains an example of a stylised flower with multiple petals, adapted from a Thomas Lester draft. Working the petals will help illustrate several points of technique: a. the gimp as a means for adding pairs (at pin-holes *1-3, 5-7 & 9-11*); b. working a nook-pin to hold the gimp in position on the narrow curve between petals (at pin-holes *4, 8 & 12*); c. the nook-pin as a point where a worker becomes a passive and provides an extra pair to fill a gap in the clothwork — a technique used also in Bucks Point.

The pattern markings are given in Fig 44a. Follow Figs 44b-c.

Begin the flower at pin-holes *1, 5 & 9*, as shown. Place the gimp between the two sets of pairs before putting up a pin at *1*. Enclose the pin and hang another pair at *2*. Work a row and hang another pair at *3*. Work to pin-hole *4* and make a nook-pin stitch. Pass the gimp through the workers, twist three times, put up pin and pass the gimp back again through the workers. This worker pair will now become a passive.

As the next pin-hole to be worked is pin-hole *5*, hang two extra pairs on the gimp in preparation for pin *7*. Take the gimp through the feeder pairs for pin-hole *5*, work a cloth stitch with the two centre pairs, put up pin *5*, enclose the pin and work towards pin-hole *6*.

Hang on a new pair at pin-hole *6*. Work back to pin-hole *7* taking in one of the two pairs left hanging on the gimp after pin-hole *4*. Leave the other extra pair in abeyance until the continuous row all the way across needs to be worked. This pair will help fill holes which often form underneath pin-holes *4, 8 & 12*.

Follow these instructions for the other upper petals, working across the entire top of the flower until the top pin-hole of the inner circle is reached.

These long rows can seem very unwieldy and will remain so until you reach the top pin-hole of the inner circle. When you reach this point pull all passives down carefully into position and, making sure that enough pairs are retained to work the centre filling, lay back extra pairs. See Removing pairs p 13.

You can lay a gimp at this point to emphasise the centre. Centres of flowers come with a variety of fillings which often match the ground. See Grounds and Pls 8 & 18.

Continue working the flower with the appropriate centre filling.

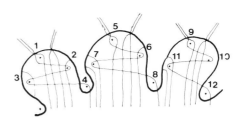

44b. Beginning the petals. Numbers show the order of setting in (wd/p).

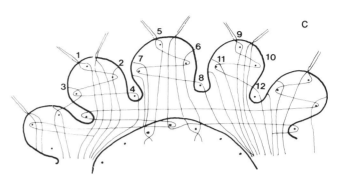

44c. Working across the top of the flower and dividing for the centre (wd/p).

The Honiton rose Fig 45, Pl 7

The significant influence of Honiton lace on the designers of East Midlands lace is marked by the inclusion of the Honiton Rose motif into Bedfordshire patterns. This required particular skills by lace-makers because it involved handling many pairs of workers meeting at joint pin-holes at the edges of numerous petals. An example of this is shown in Plate 21 and Figure 43. This type of flower should be attempted only after mastering the techniques given for the previous flowers.

The flower shown has two rings of petals and can be worked either in cloth stitch throughout or in a mixture of cloth stitch and half-stitch for added contrast. Like a flower based on a simple circle, it is started at the top pin-hole, but is worked through at the same level. Each petal, however, is worked separately with its own worker pair which meet worker pairs from adjoining petals at joint pin-holes.

A gimp, laid round the outer edge of the petals will help to outline the design.

Figure 44

Flower with multiple petals

a. Pattern marking often found in designs by the firm of Lester.

Figure 45

Honiton rose

Pattern marking. The motif is occasionally found in Bedfordshire designs.

Grounds

The most common ground is made just with plaits, crossed with a windmill and decorated with picots (Pl 1, Fig 46a-d). The picots face one way (Fig 46a), two ways (Fig 46b), or they can be double (Fig 46c). The coarser Bedfordshire laces are almost exclusively made with this type of ground. In finer pieces a variety of grounds can be seen which show the relationship to other laces, notably Point ground (Pl 21) and Honeycomb ground (Pl 18a, not often seen in Bedfordshire lace) which were retained from previous periods, the others such as Diamond filling and Blossom Filling which were borrowed from Honiton lace (Pl 5a).

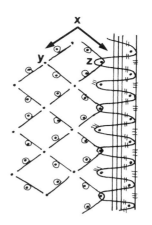

46d. Ground and footside. Lines in the ground represent plaits (two pairs); those in the footside pairs. Letters indicate order of working the ground and joining the footside.

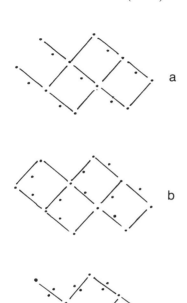

Figure 46

Plaited ground

a-c. Pattern markings showing different arrangements of picots.

Plaited ground with picots facing two ways Fig 46d, Pl 1

Begin with 4 pairs at *x*. With the left two pairs work a half-stitch plait long enough to reach the picot hole. Work a left-hand picot and continue to pin-hole *y*. With the two right-hand pairs from *x* work a half-stitch plait long enough to reach the picot hole. Work a left-hand picot and continue the plait to *z*.

Joining to the footside. Work the footside workers through the two plait pairs, twist and put up pin, work back through the plait pairs and leave them out to return to the ground. Use the workers to continue the edge. To cross the plaits work a windmill.

Plaited ground with raised tally at the crossing Fig 46e, Pl 4

In some pieces of lace, seen in museums, the crossings of plaits are decorated with raised tallies. Instead of working ordinary windmill crossings work as follows.

Using the two centre pairs, work a half-stitch, put up pin, enclose pin with a half-stitch and with these two centre pairs make a tally. Lay it back.

With the two outside pairs work a cloth stitch and twist and put the pairs to the side.

Bring down the tally into position, propping it up and re-pinning. See Tallies, p 14. Continue working half-stitch plaits with the two left-hand and the two right-hand pairs.

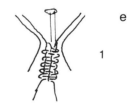

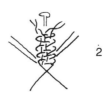

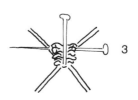

Fig 46e. Working a raised tally on a Windmill crossing in a plaited ground. Stages of working: 1, making the tally; 2, laying the tally to the back; 3, propping the tally into position after the crossing.

Plate 1

Edging with a feather-shaped scalloped headside, cloth stitch circles in a plaited ground and oblong cucumber tallies in the footside. The pricking shows an extra thick marking down the central line of circles, indicating a larger number of pairs in the joining plaits. See detail.

Worked by Mrs Vi Bullard from a pricking in the collection of Mrs W Millar.

Detail

Note the extra pair in the plaits connecting the cloth stitch circles. Nine extra pairs were needed to fill the clothwork area in each head.

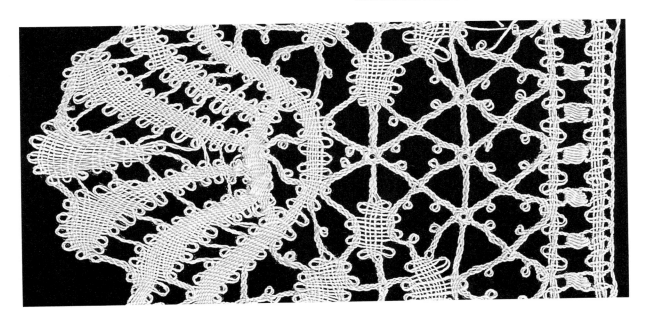

Plate 2

Edging with a deep scalloped headside, ninepin edge and motif of a stylised leaf worked in cloth stitch. The sample also shows the use of trails in the composition of the design.

Worked by Mrs Vi Bullard from a pricking in the collection of Mrs W Millar.

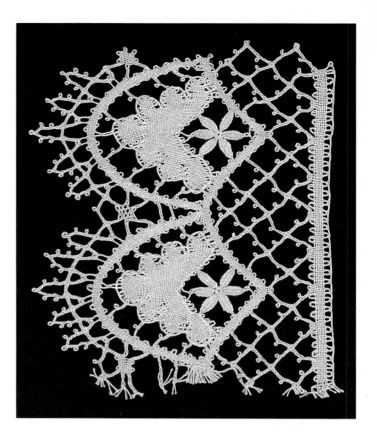

Detail

Note the stylised leaf motif in the headside where nine extra pairs were needed to work the clothwork area.

Plate 3

Collar or yoke: the design shows a variety of motifs including a naturalistic rose flower with a Point ground centre, and veined leaf motifs. Added interest and texture were obtained by flat overlaid tallies and gimps.

Worked by the author from a parchment stamped C&T L (Charles and Thomas Lester) in the collection of Mrs S King.   Thread: 100 linen.

Plate 3, continued

Back section of the collar showing the
variety of motifs and design units. The
neckline was on the right-hand side of
the pattern, as a footside.

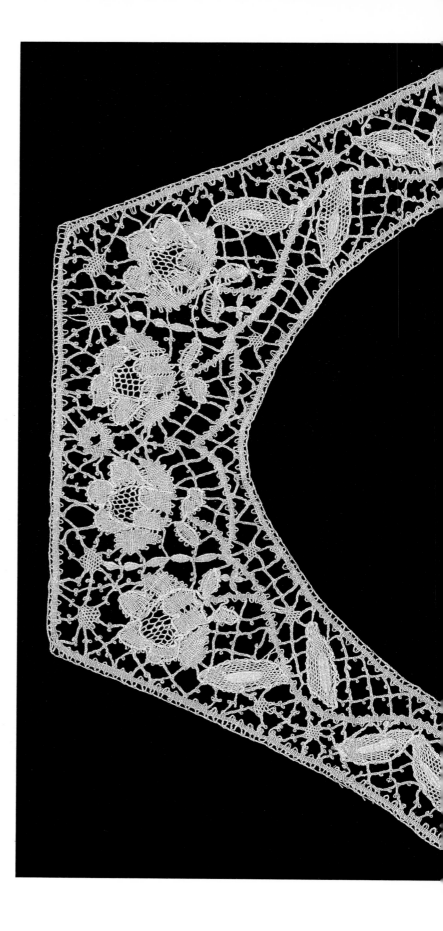

Plate 3, detail
Note the Point ground centre of the
flower.

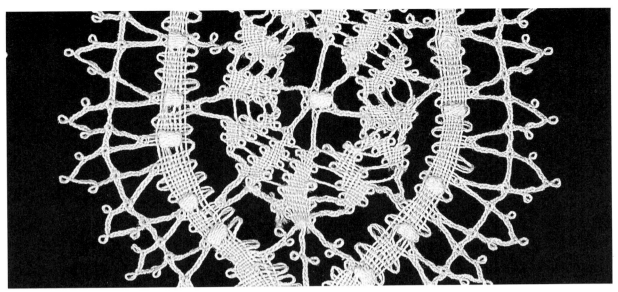

Plate 4

Dress cap with elaborate design, pointed front, three separate tails at the back and a variety of motifs and components including the 'wheel', a raised tally at a Windmill crossing, trails set at different positions and decorated with raised tallies. *Opposite page*, slightly reduced. *Left*, shown as worn.

  Worked by Mrs Sue Willoughby from a pricking in the collection of Mrs V Bullard.   Thread: 50 Madeira Tanne.

Above, detail

Note the use of raised tallies on the trail and the half-stitch bud in the centre of the veined circle.

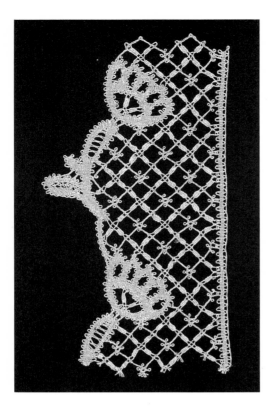

Plate 5

Sample, showing a combined Plaited
ground and Blossom filling. The picots in
the Blossom filling were worked in the
Honiton manner.

  Worked by the author; adapted from a
draft inscribed 'Lester' in the collection
of Luton Museum.   Thread: Madeira
Tanne 80.

Plate 5a, above right

Edging with scrolled trail in the
headside, a cluster of holes in the
clothwork forming a stylised leaf. The
loops of the double ninepin edge are
joined by a kiss stitch. The Honiton
Blossom filling is worked in the
Bedfordshire manner.

  Worked by Mrs Sandra King; pricking
adapted from a draft, *right,* inscribed
'Lester' in the collection of Luton
Museum.   Thread: Brok 80/2.

40

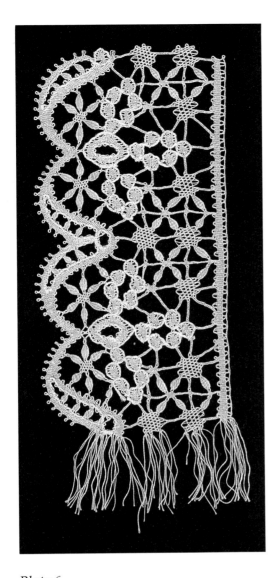

Plate 6

Edging with extensive use of gimps
round cloth stitch areas. The scalloped
headside is in the form of a stylised leaf
or cone motif edged with picots, showing
the influence of Point ground. The
design also shows an example of a simple
flower made up of pointed tallies.

    Worked by Mrs Sandra King; pricking
adapted from a draft, *above,* inscribed
'Lester' in the collection of Luton
Museum.   Thread: Brok 80/2.

Plate 7

Collar, showing how a
Honiton rose was
incorporated into a
Bedfordshire pattern and
worked in Bedfordshire
techniques. The outer edge
or headside is formed by the
flower petals. Made in three
pieces, two lapels and the
neckband.

Worked by Mrs Shelagh
Thornber from a pricking in
the collection of Mrs V
Bullard. Thread: Brok
cotton; the lapels in 80/2, the
neckband in 60/2.

Detail, opposite page
The flower petals were
defined in cloth stitch and
half-stitch and each petal is
outlined by a gimp.

42

Plate 8

Edging showing a combination of Point ground and Honiton design features in a Bedfordshire pattern, *below*, dated 1856 and inscribed 'Lester'. The circular flower motif with multiple petals is often found in Lester designs.

Worked by Mrs Mrs Sandra King; pricking adapted from a draft in the collection of Luton Museum.   Thead: Madeira Tanne 50.

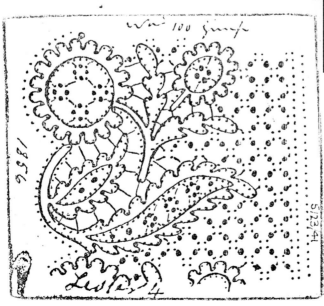

44

Detail

Note the combination of the Honiton Diamond filling used as a Plaited ground and the Honiton Four Tallies filling in the flower and leaf motifs. The picot edgings on the headside and the outlining gimp have been adopted from Point ground to great effect.

Plate 9

Collar with a cone (Paisley) design. The loose open structure held together with half-stitch buds in places typifies much Bedfordshire lace design at the turn of the century, when speed of working was essential.

Worked by the author from a pricking in her collection.   Thread: DMC 50 Retors d'Alsace.

46

Plate 10

Collar with ivy leaf motifs illustrating the use of naturalistic features in lace design, a trend which developed during the second half of the 19th century. The collar is bordered by a double, overlapping ninepin edge. The leaves intrude into the ninepin forming part of the edge itself.

Worked by the author from a pricking in the collection of Mrs V Bullard.   Thread: 140 linen.

Plate 10, continued

This page; section, showing the beginning of a collar with a deep front point, set in at a ninepin edge.

Detail, opposite page
Note the different position of leaves and veins. The veins were outlined by a gimp of Coton à Broder 16. Tallies were worked with pointed ends to provide more space between them.

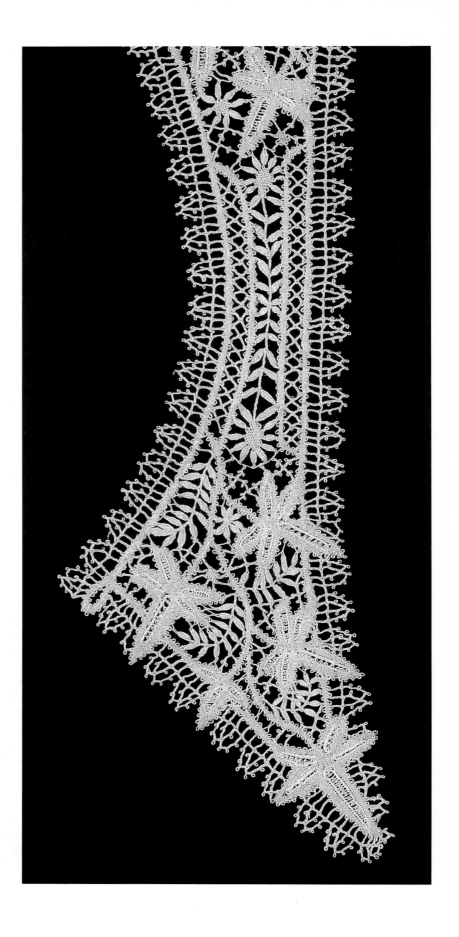

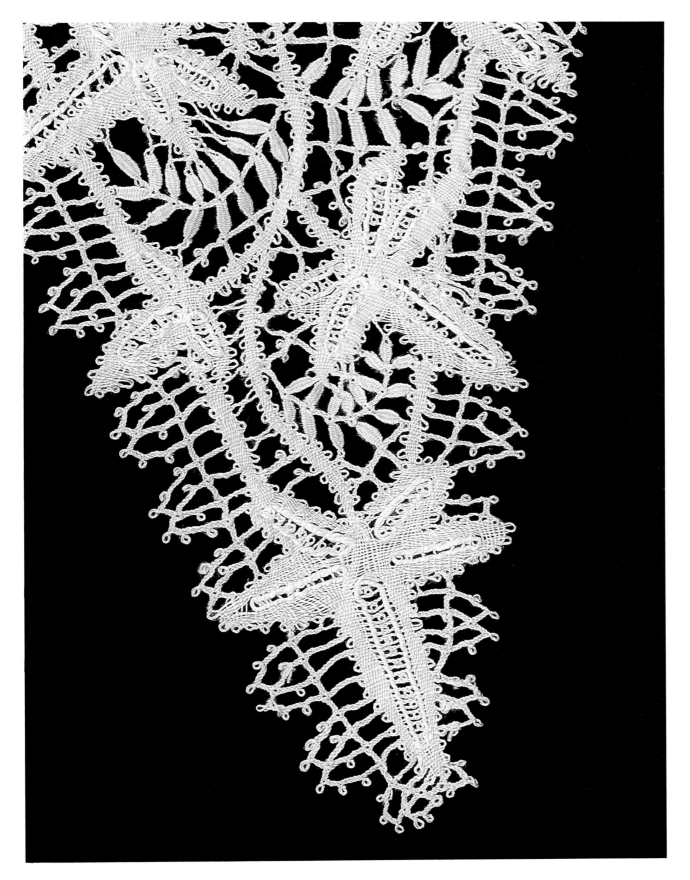

Plate 11 is on page 54

Plate 12

Circular motif with a variety of trails,
joins between trails set close together
and several types of filling. The gimp is
laid outside the pins as in Point ground.

Worked by Mrs Jackie Poulter. The
motif was taken and adapted from a
parchment for a mantle in the collection
of Mrs V Bullard. Mrs Poulter worked
the motif all the way round like a circular
edging rather than across from top to
bottom as would have been done in the
original.   Thread: Madeira Tanne 80.

Detail, opposite page
Note the use of the
cucumber tallies to form links between
parallel trails. The gimp was laid outside
the pins as in Point ground.

Plate 13

Cuff showing an edge of oval motifs with densely worked raised tallies.

Worked by Mrs Sue Goodman. The original parchment, in the collection of Mrs V Bullard, was enlarged by 15% because both threads and pins available nowadays are too thick to work the original. Thread: Brok cotton 80/2.

Detail, opposite page
A close-up of the densely worked raised tallies.

52

Plate 11

Hanging pieces or lappets for a cap, here joined and made into a tie. The original would have been worn attached to a cap as shown in an issue of the fashion magazine *The Queen* of 1868 (from *Victorian Costume and Costume Accessories* by Anne Buck). The cone (Paisley) design was a popular motif in mid-nineteenth century textiles. The scalloped ninepin edge is formed by double overlapping loops and two rows of bars. The trails, which appear to curl backwards, were started separately and then joined to the main trail like two halves of a circle.

Worked by Mrs Denise Vickery as a first effort in Bedfordshire lace from a pricking in the collection of Mrs V Bullard. Thread: Madeira Tanne 50.

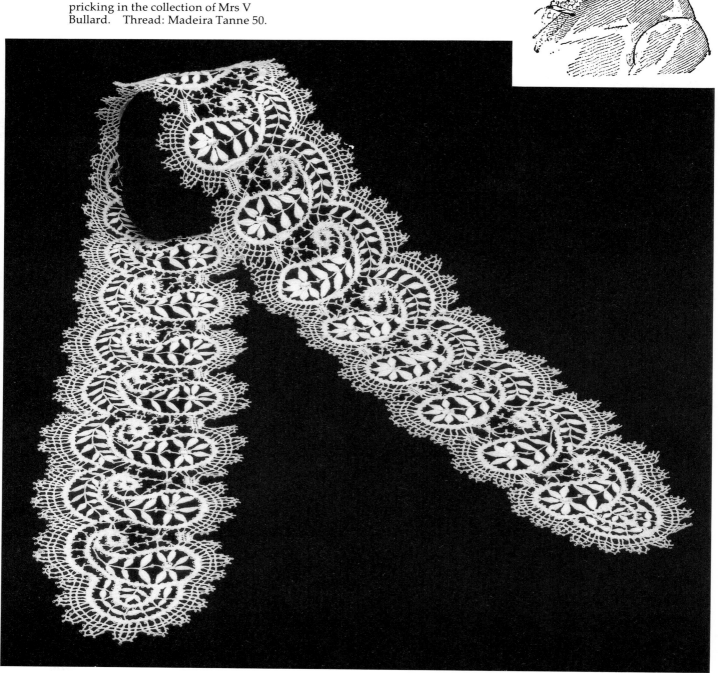

Plate 14

Edging showing an ingenious use of bars and tallies as a link between an elaborate arrangement of trails and clothwork areas. The gimp was laid round the leaf shapes in the Point ground manner and close to the passives along the trails. Note the fine Bedfordshire cloth stitch circles.

Worked by Mrs Sandra King; pricking adapted from a draft, *below*, inscribed 'Lester' in the collection of Luton Museum. Thread: DMC, 50 Retors d'Alsace.

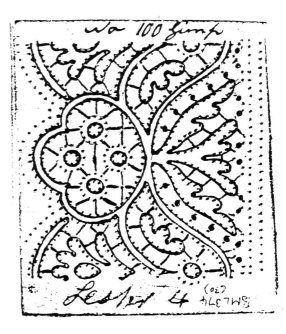

Plate 15

Handkerchief edging showing a variety
of Bedfordshire motifs, including a
flower with a raised tally on the petals.
 Worked by Mrs Sue Goodman. Origin
of pricking unknown.   Thread: Brok
cotton 100/3.

56

Detail, opposite page
Note the fine corner spray of tallies, a
tallies joining and leaving the trails.

Plate 16

Triangular insertion with a spray of
flowers and leaves. The pattern is
frequently used to practice working
veined leaves and flower petals set at
different angles.

Worked by Mrs Joan Clark as a first
attempt at Bedfordshire lace from a
pricking in the collection of Mrs V
Bullard. Thread: DMC 50 Retors
d'Alsace.

Detail, opposite page
The close-up shows the different
techniques used to outline the veins in
the flower and leaves.

59

Plate 17

Collar with a bold design of leaves decorated with raised tallies and flowers in circles. Cucumber tallies are used as part of the edging at both headside and footside. The collar featured in *The history of Wellingborough* by J and M Palmer 1972.

Worked by the author; the pricking was adapted from a parchment in the collection of Mrs W Millar.   Thread: linen 100.

Detail, opposite page
Note the technique of working a leaf and vein in two halves.

61

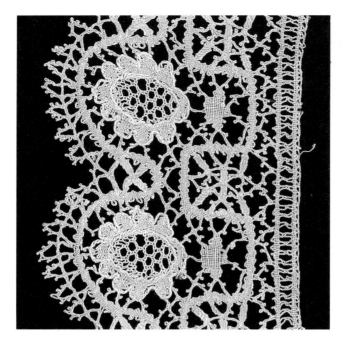

Plate 18a

Example of Honeycomb ground, here used as a filling inside the flower. Part of an old edging in the collection of the author.

Plate 18

Edging with a carnation design and an elaborate arrangement of holes in the clothwork forming a leaf motif in the headside. The carnation is a Point ground motif as is the picot edge. The ground shows two overlapping Honiton fillings: Diamond filling and Four tally filling forming a Plaited ground.

Worked by the author; pricking adapted from a draft inscribed 'Lester' in the collection of Luton Museum.   Thread: Brok 100/3

Plate 19

Oak leaves and acorns motif. The leaves were worked in blocks.

Worked by the author. Adapted from a parchment of an unfinished collar design in the collection of Mrs V Bullard.   Thread: DMC Retors d'Alsace 60.

Detail
Note the use of a gimp to help outline the
holes in clothwork forming the stylised
leaf shape.

Plate 20

Edging with corner, showing a flower with five petals and a half-stitch centre with a raised tally in the middle. It also shows an example of Flower ground, and Honiton Blossom filling, as well as a variation of a ninepin edge with two crossing bars.

Worked by the author. Adapted from a pricking attributed to the firm of Lester in the collection of Mrs W Millar. Thread: DMC 50 Retors d'Alsace.

Detail

The veins in the petals are set at different angles, petals were worked in cloth stitch and half-stitch. The Blossom filling is worked in the Honiton manner.

Plate 21

Cuff showing a fine rose and leaves design. The Point ground in the rose motif covers the entire extent of the centre with the three flower petals overlapping it, forming a second layer and giving a three dimensional effect. The cuff was worked as an attempt to reproduce the technique of a double layered centre in an identical rose displayed at the Cecil Higgins Art Gallery, Bedford.

Worked by **Mrs** Sue Willoughby; origin of pricking unknown.   Thread: Madeira Tanne 50.

Detail

The gimp is used to outline the petals, cucumber tallies form part of the footside edge and the double ninepin loops are joined with a kiss stitch.

65

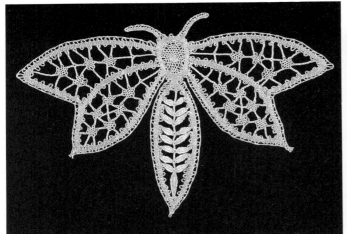

Plate 22

Moth. Butterflies, moths and other insects were popular motifs in the designs of the second half of the 19th century. This example is known amongst lace-makers as a Carnes pattern. Anne Buck in her book on Thomas Lester (p 38) points out that a number of fine patterns stamped 'A. A. Carnes', with a Bedford address, can be seen in local Museum collections. One of these was acquired from Miss Haines, who held a shop in Bedford, when she disposed of her stock. Mr Carnes collected and preserved lace patterns while working for the survival of the industry and the revival of the making of Point ground in the early years of the century. Part of his collection was presented to the town in 1924.

Note the half-stitch centre in the circular head and unconventional use of a Honiton ten stitch rib to form the antennae. The motif was started at the top and worked downwards, hanging in pairs at the sides of the head to work the wings. The finishing threads=two pairs of threads at each of the three points=were deliberately cut off to show the finishing points at the lower end of the wings and body.

Worked by the author from a pricking in the collection of Mrs W Millar.   Thread: DMC Retors d'Alsace 50.

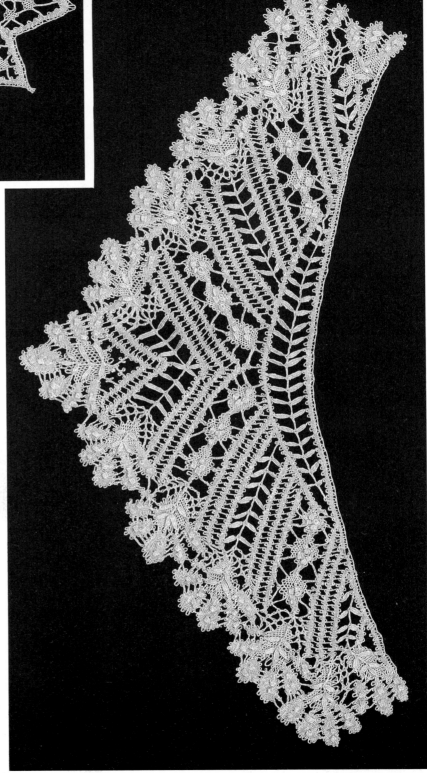

Plate 23

Cuff with elaborate arrangement of oval and striped motifs joined by twisted pairs. The pattern shows arrangements of raised and flat overlaid tallies.

Worked by Mrs Shelagh Thornber. The original parchment, in the collection of Mrs V Bullard, was enlarged by 15% to allow for threads and pins currently available.   Thread: Brok cotton 80/2.

Detail
The trail strips are linked by
twisted pairs left out of one trail to
join the one next to it.

Plate 24

Oval insertion with a variety of flower
and leaf motifs and a double trail edge.
   Worked by the author. The pattern was
taken from a large parchment in the
collection of Mrs W Millar.   Thread:
DMC 50 Retors d'Alsace.

Point ground Fig 47, Pls 3 & 21

The Point ground stitch consists of a half-stitch and two extra twists. A pin is placed between the pairs but is not enclosed. Follow Figure 47b.

To begin the ground hang one pair on each of the temporary pins *1* to *5*.

For the footside hang in a worker pair at *a*, two passive pairs and an edge pair on temporary pins. Begin with the worker pair at *a* (4th pair from edge) and work in cloth stitch towards the edge through two passive pairs. Twist the workers twice and put up edge pin *b*. With the edge pair work a cloth stitch, twisting the outer pair 3 times and the inner pair twice. Using the inner pair as a worker, work back again through the two passive pairs, twist the worker 3 times and put up pin *c*.

Joining to the footside Fig 47b-c. Make a Point ground stitch with the pair at c and the pair from 1, work a half-stitch and twist both pairs twice. Do not put up a pin. This stitch is called the *catch-pin stitch*.

Lace-makers used to say about this stitch: 'A pin without a stitch, a stitch without a pin'.

Leaving the right-hand of the two pairs at *c*, take the left-hand pair and work a Point ground stitch with the pair from temporary pin 2; put up pin *d*.

Take the left-hand pair at *d* and make a ground stitch with the pair from the temporary pin 3; put up pin at *e*. Continue to end of row. Remove temporary pins and pull the pairs down gently.

Begin each row with the 4th pair from the edge and work towards the edge as described above.

Note. If worked correctly, only the left-hand thread will have come from the footside. To check pull gently on the thread.

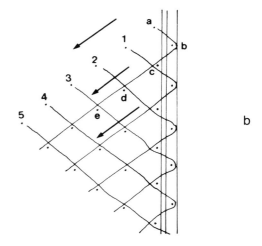

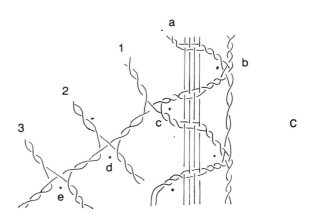

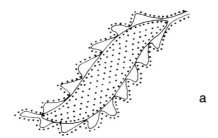

Figure 47

Point ground

a. Pattern marking inside a leaf.

b. Working the ground and footside. Nos 1-5 indicate temporary pins, pinholes *a-e* show the first row of work, and the arrows the angle of work (wd/p).

c. Detail for the first row (wd/t).

Honiton Blossom filling Fig 48a-c, Pls 5 & 20

This is another unit of design borrowed from Honiton lace. Although the pattern marking (Fig 48a) is the same as for Bedfordshire prickings, the four picots on the Honiton crossing are worked on both plaits in the order shown by the lettering on Fig 48d. The four picots on the Bedfordshire crossing are worked on the same plait: two before, and two after the crossing (see below). A crossing in the Honiton Blossom filling is worked as follows.

Beginning with the left of the two plaits (marked with an arrow), work a right-hand picot at *a* and then, with the two left-hand pairs, work a cloth stitch. With two centre pairs, work a cloth stitch and twist. With the two right-hand pairs work a cloth stitch and, with the right-hand pair, make a right-hand picot at *b*.

Work a cloth stitch with the two right-hand pairs; then a cloth stitch with the two left-hand pairs, and with the left-hand of these make a left picot at *c*. With the two left-hand pairs work a cloth stitch and work a raised tally at this point, if required. Twist the centre pairs once and work a cloth stitch. Use the two right-hand pairs to work a cloth stitch and the left-hand pair of these to make a left picot at *d*.

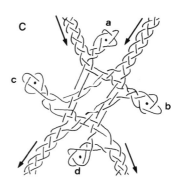

Fig 48c.   Detail of crossing (wd/t).

Make plaits with two right-hand pairs and two left-hand pairs.

Joining to the footside Fig 48b.   Work as far as pin-hole *b* and, with the footside workers, instead of working a picot work a cloth stitch and twist, enclose pin and continue.

This is the same method as used for the Honiton ground proper, but with fewer twists because of the thicker thread used for Bedfordshire lace.

Bedfordshire Blossom ground Fig 48d, Pl 5a

When the East Midlands lace designers included Honiton fillings as a ground in their lace patterns, they left local lace-makers to work out their own techniques. We therefore have an alternative *Bedfordshire* method in which, the four picots at the crossing are worked on only one of the two incoming plaits, in the order shown by the lettering on Figure 48d. Also, a windmill is worked in the centre of the crossing. Proceed as follows.

Put an extra pin-hole in the centre of the set of 4 pin-holes (for the windmill crossing). Make the left-hand plait long enough to reach the centre pin-hole. Make the right-hand plait long enough to reach pin-hole a. Make a left-hand picot at *a*; work a half-stitch with the two pairs and make a right-hand picot at *b*. Work a half-stitch with the two pairs.

With the plaits, work a windmill at the centre pin-hole; with the right-hand pairs work a picot at *c*. Work a half-stitch with the other pair of the plait and a left-hand picot at *d*. Continue working the plaits until the next crossing.

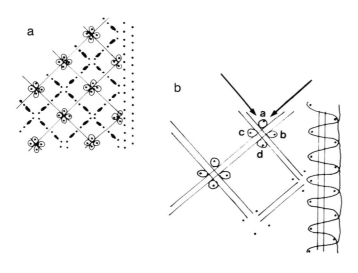

Figure 48

Blossom filling and Blossom ground

a.   Pattern marking for combined Blossom and Diamond filling.

48b.   Blossom filling, with picots at the crossing worked in the Honiton manner, in the order as shown by the letters (wd/p).

Joining to the footside Fig 48d. The join between the ground and the footside is worked with two pairs of a plait and the footside worker.

Work the plait to pin-hole e and make a right-hand picot, then work a half-stitch with the same two pairs. Join the right-hand pair with the footside worker in a cloth stitch and twist, put up pin and enclose it. With the two top plait pairs work a cloth stitch and twist; then make a left picot, work a half-stitch, make a right picot and continue.

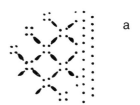

Figure 49

Honiton Diamond filling

a.   Pattern marking.

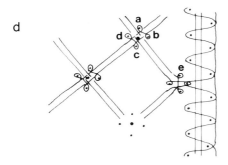

Fig 48d.   Blossom filling worked in the Bedfordshire manner. The picots at the crossing are worked in a different order, shown by the letters (wd/p).

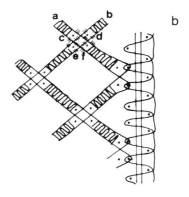

49b.   Letters indicate the order of working for the crossing; note the join to the footside (wd/p).

Honiton Diamond filling or Plaited ground   Fig 49, Pl 8

Follow Figures 49b-c. Twist each of the two pairs at *a* & *b* three times and make a narrow square-ended tally long enough to reach pins *c* & *d* (respectively). Put up pins *c* & *d*. Twist each pair three times.

With the two centre pairs work a cloth stitch and twist each three times. With each of the two side pairs work a cloth stitch and twist all pairs three times. Work a cloth stitch again with the centre pairs and twist them three times. Put up pins *e* & *f* in readiness for the next two tallies. Pull up firmly.

Joining to the footside Fig 49b.   Work a tally from *f*. Twist each pair three times. With the right-hand pair from the tally and the footside worker work a whole stitch, put up pin and enclose it. Twist the tally pair three times and work a cloth stitch with the left-hand tally pair; twist both pairs three times and join with the footside worker at its next footside pin-hole. Twist this pair three times and put up pin to start the next tally.

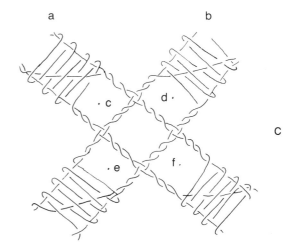

49c.   Detail for the crossing (wd/t).

Four tally ground or filling   Fig 50, and Pl 18

The four tally filling has also been borrowed from Honiton lace, where it is used mostly as a centre filling for flower motifs.

Follow Fig 50b. There will be two pairs each at pins *a* & *b*. With the two centre pairs make a cucumber tally between these pins.

With each of the outer pairs, at pin-holes *a* and *b*, work a narrow square-ended tally long enough to reach pin-holes *c* & *d*. Put up pin and work a cucumber between *c* & *d* matching that between *a* & *b*.

Plait the left-hand pairs (from *c*) together to reach *e*. Plait together the right-hand pairs (from *d*) to reach *f*.

Joining to the footside Fig 50b. Use the workers from the footside and the right-hand pair from the plait to make a horizontal cucumber tally. Continue working the footside. Work a square-ended tally from *f* to *g*. With the workers from the footside and the right-hand pair from the tally at g work another cucumber tally. Continue working in the direction of the arrows.

Honeycomb ground   Fig 51, Pl 18a

This is one of the most common mesh stitches used in Point ground laces, where it is usually found at the headside, as a filling enclosed by clothwork; it rarely joins the footside.

Each unit of mesh is worked in two stages: first a long row (in this case pin-holes *1* to *6*) and then a short row (*a* to *c*). Both rows are worked in the same honeycomb stitch, as follows (Fig 51b-c):

Work a half-stitch and one extra twist,
Put up pin between the pairs,
Enclose the pin with a half-stitch and one extra twist.

Having worked the first row, *1* to *6*, join pairs, two at a time, at pin-holes *a-c* (Fig 51b), as follows:

Work pairs from *1* & *2* to pin-hole *a*,
Work pairs from *3* & *4* to pin-hole *b*,
Work pairs from *5* & *6* to pin-hole *c*.

The line between pin-holes *1* to *6* also indicates the angle at which the stitches are worked in relation to the footside.

Figure 51

Honeycomb ground

a.   Pattern marking.

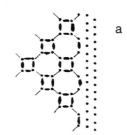

Figure 50

Four tally ground

a.   Pattern marking.

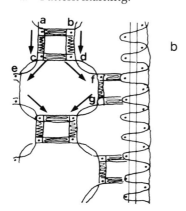

50b.   Working a unit of ground and joining to the footside. Arrows and letters show the order of working (wd/p).

51b.   The mesh is completed in two rows, a long row (pin-holes 1-6) and a short row (pin-holes *a-c*). The arrow along the ground shows the direction of working (wd/p).

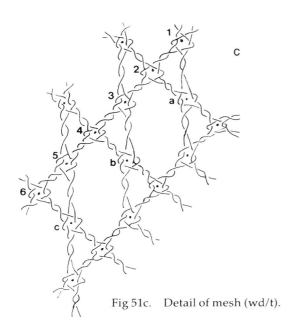

Fig 51c.   Detail of mesh (wd/t).

Joining to the footside Fig 51b.   To join the ground to the footside, work a honeycomb stitch at the footside pin-holes.

Flower ground   Fig 52, Pl 20

This ground is a mixture of plaits and tallies forming flowers with half-stitch centres, often found in the patterns of Thomas Lester. It is advisable to make the tallies quite bulbous so that they stand out from the surrounding plaits. Follow Figure 52b.

At each flower, work first the four upper tallies (*1* to *4*). With the pairs from the tallies, work a half-stitch centre and leave out two pairs at each of the four lower pin-holes (*5* to *8*). Put up a pin at the end of each of these tallies and continue working a plait with each of the pairs.

Take the pair from plait *5* horizontally to form tally *1* of the next flower, and so on round the flower, as shown.

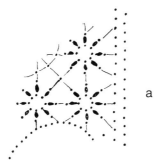

Figure 52

Flower ground

a.   Pattern marking.

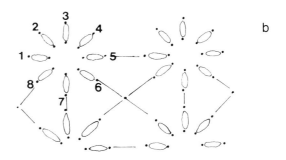

52b.   Working diagram; numbers show order of working. Straight lines indicate plaits.

Beginning and finishing

JOINING EDGINGS

Before starting a length of lace which must be joined to itself, e.g. a handkerchief edging, the line of the join must be considered very carefully. The following points should be borne in mind.

1. It is easier to begin with solid areas of cloth-work and end with the plaits that feed into them.

2. A diagonal or staggered join line across the lace will be less noticeable than a straight one.

3. Just before or just after a corner is often a convenient position for a join.

4. Look for the area with the smallest amount of ground between the headside and the footside at which to start the lace. Large areas of ground are difficult to join.

5. If you do have to join areas of ground it will be easier to do so on a diagonal start line.

When the appropriate length has been worked, pin the beginning of the lace into position against the end of the lace on the pillow. Work the join as follows.

With the pairs travelling in the same direction as if the work is to be continued, hook one of the two threads of a pair through the loop matching its position on the beginning edge. Pass its pair through the loop thus formed, pull all firm and tie together.

In some cases it will be necessary to thread these ends into a needle and weave them into the cloth-work. In other cases it will be possible to oversew the ends neatly together.

In the past, lace-makers would work about half an inch extra on the footside and trails and tie all the passives across with reef knots. They would then darn all the ends in neatly, or just use the worker pairs to sew everything together. The plaits were either tied together and the ends sewn in or darned together.

Beginnings

A collar is normally started at the left-hand front tip or fastening point and worked round, treating the inner neckline as the footside and the outer edge as the headside. The place to begin a collar will depend on its shape at the front. There are three main shapes, which are shown in Figure 53. Some collars will have to be started in two directions at once. For this two methods of hanging in are given, depending on the type of edge in the collar, one for a ninepin edge and the other for a straight edge.

Collar a. The front edge is cut away sharply. It must be started at that point and widened gradually towards its outer edge as shown by the arrows (Fig 53a).

Collar b. The ends in Collar *b* are almost rectangular, so it will have to be started at *x* and worked in two directions simultaneously. An example is the collar in Pl 9. The actual hanging in of pairs for working in two directions will depend on the type of edge. See p 75.

Set in at *x* for working in two directions, as appropriate for the particular edge and follow the arrows. Work the front edge of the collar first, hanging in pairs from this edge so that passives hang in the direction shown by the three arrows. When you have reached the full width of the collar at the front edge, work in the direction shown by the arrows, using the inner neck line as a footside and working at 90° to it.

Collar c. This type of collar has a deep front point and it too will have to be started at point *x* and worked in two directions as shown by the arrows. The largest number of pairs will be required across the front points, on a line between *y* and a point on the outer edge.

Widen the work gradually towards *y*. At *y* the edge will change into a footside and the work will narrow quickly to form the curve of the neckline. Turn the pillow at this point to continue the work in the direction of the arrows.

At the same time, work the outer edge in the direction of the arrows until it too can be worked at 90° to the footside (inner neckline).

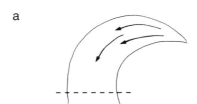

Figure 53

Working collars with different shapes

a. Collar with a sharply curved front. It is started at the front point and widens gradually in the direction of the arrows.

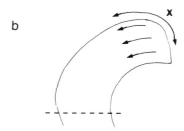

53b. Collar with an almost rectangular front. It is started at *x* and worked in two directions simultaneously.

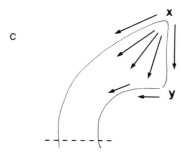

53c. Collar with deep front point. It too must be started at *x* and worked in two directions. At *y* the outer edge becomes the footside and forms the curve of the neckline.

Collar endings

Unless a collar is made in two matching halves, the pricking will usually consist of a half which extends a little beyond the back centre line. When the end of the centre back section is completed the lace-maker must either use a reverse pricking or turn the original pricking upside-down, having first marked the under side to match the first half, to work the second half.

When turning a pricking for use as the second half of a collar, rub the surface with a hard but smooth object in order to flatten well the used pin-holes.

When a very complicated pattern needs to be reversed and matching it up may be difficult, a join at a convenient spot is worth considering. This can be somewhere at the back or the side of the collar — especially if the design narrows at the side, as in the collar on Pl 10.

With collars *a* and *b* you will work all the way round in one go, starting at one front fastening point and finishing at the other. As you work round towards the end try and remove as many pairs as possible into the trail at the neck edge, while working the instructions for the beginning in reverse order.

Collars with pointed ends, as in *c*, will be completed differently. Work all the way round to point *x* removing pairs at the pin-holes at which they had been added for the beginning.

On many old collars (such as types *a* & *b*) the trail or footside was continued for about half an inch at the neck, tied off and folded under the lace as an easy way to finish. It also provided extra support for pinning a brooch.

HANGING IN TO WORK IN TWO DIRECTIONS AT ONCE

Sometimes the beginning of a collar or any other piece of lace, involves setting in on the edge of the pattern and working in two directions at once. The method of hanging in pairs will vary with the type of edge to be worked. Two of the most common edges are the ninepin and the straight edge.

At a ninepin edge   Fig 54a-c, Pl 10

Follow Fig 54b. Hang two pairs round pin *1*, twist them three times.

Anchor the four ninepin pairs (for the loop plaits) at temporary pin *a*. Anchor the four ninepin pairs (for the bar) at temporary pin *b*.

With the pairs from *a* and *b* work a windmill at pin *4*. Plait the pairs to reach pin *5* and *1* respectively.

With the pairs from pin *4* work in cloth stitch through the left-hand pair hanging at pin *1* and work through the right-hand pair hanging at pin *1*.

With these two pairs from pin *1* continue and plait to pin *5*; with the plait from *4* work a windmill at pin *5*.

Anchor one end of each of six pairs at *c*. These will be the *trail passives*, so lay them accordingly in position on the pattern.

With the left-hand pair hanging from *1* work through the trail passives in cloth stitch and put up pin *2*.

With the right-hand pair from pin *1* work through the trail passives in cloth stitch and put up pin *3*, as shown. The pair that worked through to pin *2* will be the *worker* pair for the trail working towards *the left*.

The right-hand pair that worked through to pin *3* will be the trail *worker* pair working towards *the right*.

Remove temporary pins *a-c* and continue, adding picots as required, as shown in Fig 54c.

Figure 54

Hanging in to work in two directions at once at a ninepin curve or point

a.   Pattern marking.

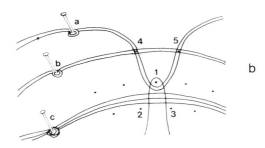

54b.   Hanging in. Pairs anchored at temporary pin *a* will be the loop plaits, those at *b* will be the bar plaits and those at *c* the trail passives. From pin-hole 1 the two worker pairs separate to work to the left, to pin-hole 2; and to the right, to pin-hole 3 (wd/p).

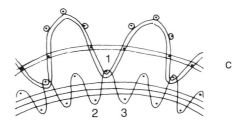

54c.   Working diagram showing a section of a ninepin edge (wd/p).

At an edge pair   Fig 55

This type of beginning is used for corners on collars, insertions or other pieces of lace where straight edges meet at a point as in Pl 3 & 16. Figure 55a is an example of a pattern marking.

Two ways of hanging in the first four pairs are given.

Method I Fig 55b-c. Hang four pairs open on the top pin *c*, twist the two left pairs twice; then work a cloth stitch with the two right-hand pairs and twist them twice. Continue following Fig 55c.

Anchor eight pairs to one side of the pillow. Work through them with both pairs of workers, put up pin *x* and take the workers *round* pin *x* from the different directions and back to their respective sides. This is the same as if you were working a footside.

If two further pairs need to be hung on pin *x* (to work a plait or tally), it will be easier to hang one pair from each of the next two pin-holes, *y* & *z* and twist them until they can join to start the plait.

Method II Fig 55c.   Hang two pairs on each temporary pin *a* & *b* above the work. Make a windmill crossing with them at pin-hole *c*. Remove temporary pins and pull down into position.

With the two pairs on the left work a cloth stitch and twist the pairs three times. Do the same with the two pairs on the right. The two outer pairs will be the edge pairs: one working to the left, the other to the right of pin-hole c. The two inner pairs will be the workers for either side of pin-hole c.

Continue by laying the six passive pairs for the trail across the pillow, anchoring them on the side, as described in the previous method.

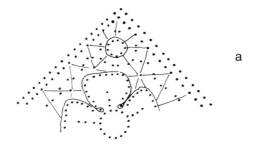

Figure 55

Hanging in to work in two directions at once at a straight edge

a.   Pattern marking.

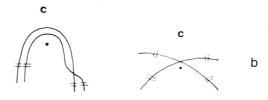

55b.   Hanging in with four pairs open on pin *c*, following Method I.

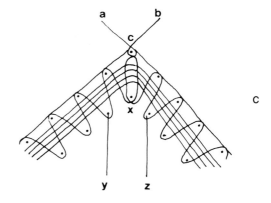

55c.   Method II. *a* & *b* are temporary pins which are removed after a windmill crossing is worked at pin *c*. In both methods the first four pairs form edge pairs and workers, which then work in different directions. Extra pairs can be hung on pins at *y* & *z* if required.

READING AND RE-DRAFTING OLD PATTERNS

Old parchments should be preserved rather than used for actual lace-making. If they are well used they are likely to be inaccurate, and if they are not used it would be a shame to spoil them,especially since they are no longer difficult to reproduce.

Often the markings have been worn off by constant use and it may be difficult to see just where the joins of half-stitch plaits should be. Picots, too, will often have 'strayed' a long way away from the plait.

Sometimes photocopies can be made, but here again, unless it is an original designer's draft, care must be taken to check that it is a usable pattern: large parchments can be distorted by a photocopier and the photocopying process itself may harm old brittle parchments. Some parchments have had a main feature cut out, and only very occasionally will this part still be attached to the main pattern; this was a way of preserving the 'copyright' on a pattern used by lace-dealers. So there is certainly a need to check the design before assuming a usable pricking.

An example of re-drafting is given in Figures 56. First of all the pattern must be 'read' (Fig 56b). This means looking for the shapes of flowers, leaves and trails. Once they are established, the next step is to see what joins them together — a close filling or simple plaits with or without picots. The picot pin-holes are often marked so far away from the plait that they can distract from seeing the basic design.

Having decided the nature of the design, use sheets of heavy tracing paper to reconstruct the pricking in stages (Fig 56c). First draw an outline of the main features, then proceed to fill in the edging and fillings, on further sheets if necessary (Fig 56d).

If the pattern is a series of repeats, only one 'head' needs to be drawn in accurately with all its detail. This can then be photocopied and the required number of heads joined together to give the full length.

When the main features have been traced, the straight lines made straight, the curved lines made regular, etc., re-trace the design very lightly in pencil. Replace it on top of the original source and mark the pin-holes, making them more even and regular where necessary (Fig 56e). In some types of lace, where regularity is essential, a grid is necessary to plot the pin-holes; for Bedfordshire lace patterns, the eye is the best judge and can achieve a more natural effect.

Normally it is easier to mark the positions of zig-zag plaits after all the other features are seen to be correct. The positions of picots can be marked last of all.

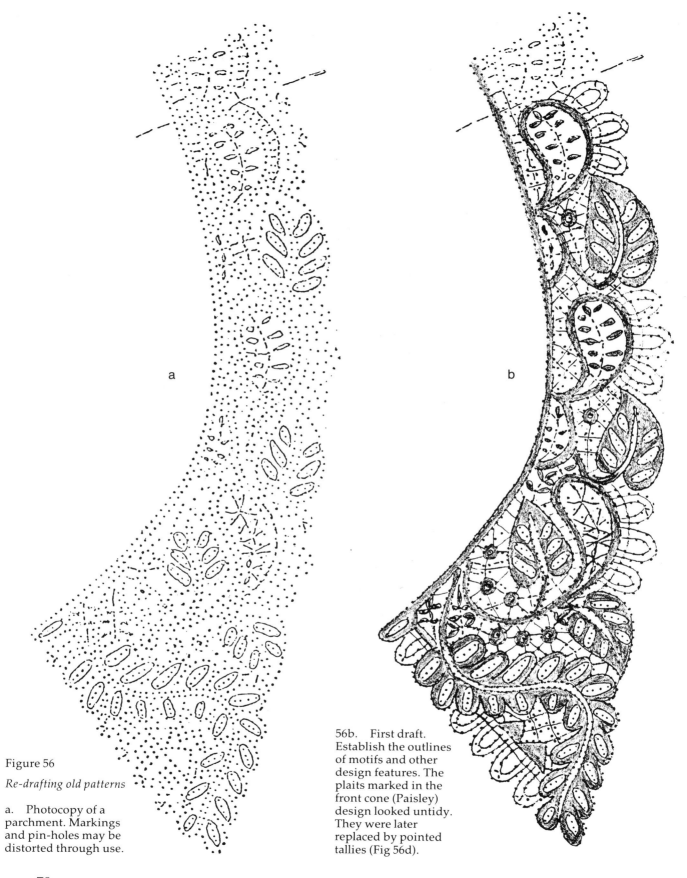

a

b

Figure 56

Re-drafting old patterns

a.　Photocopy of a
parchment. Markings
and pin-holes may be
distorted through use.

56b.　First draft.
Establish the outlines
of motifs and other
design features. The
plaits marked in the
front cone (Paisley)
design looked untidy.
They were later
replaced by pointed
tallies (Fig 56d).

78

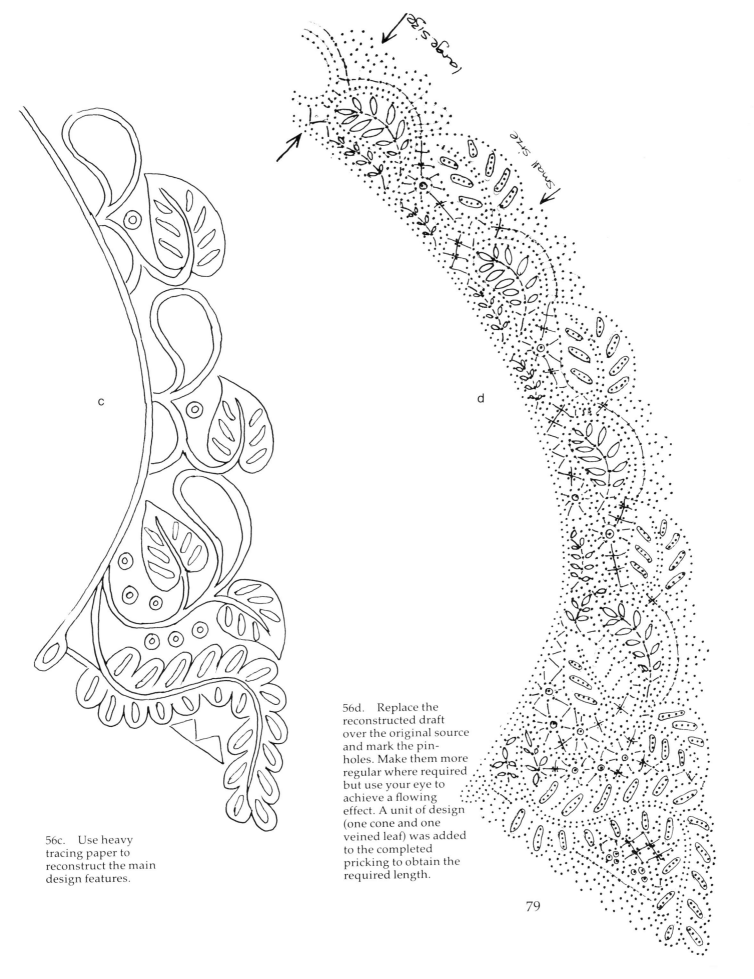

c

d

(large size)

Small size

56c. Use heavy tracing paper to reconstruct the main design features.

56d. Replace the reconstructed draft over the original source and mark the pin-holes. Make them more regular where required but use your eye to achieve a flowing effect. A unit of design (one cone and one veined leaf) was added to the completed pricking to obtain the required length.

79

GLOSSARY

Bar (*bride*, leg, plait) — braid made with four threads. In Bedfordshire lace bars are used to fill in areas within, and between, parts of the design. They can be decorated with Picots (see below).

Barleycorn — old Bedfordshire term for a square-ended, straight-sided Tally (see below).

Blocking — method of working areas of cloth stitch between the veins of leaves or flowers (see p 25).

Bride — see Bar.

Close or enclose — the working of the second half of a stitch after a pin had been put up.

Clothwork (*toile*) — area of lace worked in cloth stitch giving the effect of woven cloth. Here used synonymously with area of half-stitch.

Cucumber — a connecting Tally (see below) worked with the weavers from two parallel trails (see p 14).

Filling — term derived from Honiton lace where it denotes stitches used to fill areas within motifs, e.g. Diamond filling. Sometimes used in Bedfordshire for Ground (see below).

Footside (footing) — the straight (inner) edge of the lace where it can be joined to other material. In English laces the footside is worked on the right-hand side.

Gaining on a pin — using a pin-hole twice in order to maintain the angle between the workers and the footside at 90°.

Gimp — a thick, soft thread which serves to outline parts of the design (see p 18).

Ground — the area of lace between the headside with its motifs and the footside. The term originally denoted the undecorated mesh of all East Midland lace and continues to be used for Bucks Point *ground*. With the introduction of the Maltese type lace and fillings from Honiton lace Bedfordshire ground became formed with plaits and tallies respectively.

Half-stitch — lace-making stitch in which only one thread of the worker pair traverses the passive threads (see Fig 3), giving the lace a more open appearance.

Headpin — Bedfordshire term for a Picot (see below).

Headside (heading) — outer edge of the lace, opposite to the footside. In English lace it is worked on the left-hand side of the pricking.

Lay back — to discard unwanted threads by laying them to the back of the pillow, to be cut off when the pins are removed.

Legs — Bedfordshire term for *brides*, bars or plaits.

Ninepin — an arrangement of plaits (bars or legs) forming a characteristic outer edge for Bedfordshire lace, from the mid-19th century onwards (see p 8).

Nook-pin — a stitch that holds the gimp in position (see p 19).

Overlaid (flat) tallies — tallies lying flat on top of areas of clothwork (see p 16). Also called 'long spots' in Bedfordshire.

Parchment — treated animal skin, used for prickings because of its durability. The term is still used to denote a lace pattern even though glazed card is now the normal material.

Passives — the threads hanging down on the pillow, i.e. not the workers. In weaving terms the passives would be the warp.

Picots (headpins) — decorative loops made on the headside of the lace or on plaits (see p 5).

Plaits (legs or bars) — a continuous half-stitch worked with four threads making a bar. In parts of Bedfordshire this term is also used to denote tallies, wheatears and barleycorns.

Plaited lace or ground — A term used in Bedfordshire to refer to both the ground made with bars or plaits, with or without picots, and that made with tallies, adopted from Honiton lace such, as Diamond filling (see Pl 8).

Raised tally (spot) — small knobs worked onto an area of clothwork to give added interest and texture.

Sewings — term used in other lace-making techniques for a join made with looped threads. Not done in traditional Bedfordshire lace.

Tally (leaf) — small solid decoration made with four threads, one thread weaving over and under the other three (see p 14).

Temporary pin — a pin placed outside the pattern to anchor a new pair while it is being incorporated.

Trail — a curving, continuous band of clothwork forming edge scallops and other features of the design.

Turning stitches — another term to describe putting up a pin and changing the direction of the worker pair.

Wheatear — leaf-shaped tally.

Windmill — a crossing of four legs or plaits (see p 6).

Worker — a pair of threads which work through the passives. In weaving terms they would be the weft.

READING LIST

Buck, A, *Thomas Lester, his Lace and the East Midlands Industry 1820-1905*, Bedford, 1981.

Bury Palliser, F, *A History of Lace*, London, 1864.

Channer, C C, *Practical Lace-making: Bucks Point-Ground*, Leicester, 1928.

Channer, C C and Roberts, J F, *Lace-making in the Midlands, past and present*, London, 1900.

Cole, A S, *Report on Northampton, Bucks and Beds Lace-making*, 1892.

Freeman, C, *Pillow Lace in the East Midlands*, Luton, 1958.

Wright, T, *The Romance of the Lace Pillow*, Olney, 1919; 2nd edition 1924: reprint Bedford, 1982.

Prickings

Prickings for Plates 1, 3, 4, 5, 7, 10 & 11 can be found on the folding sheet in the pocket at the back.

Plate 2

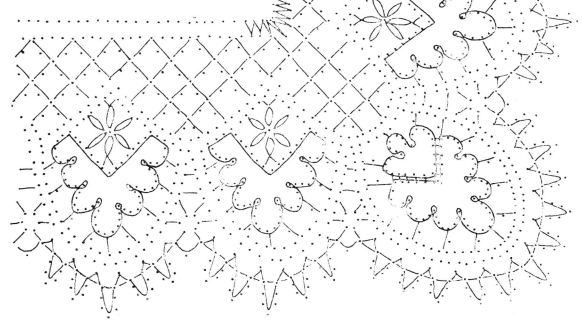

Plate 8

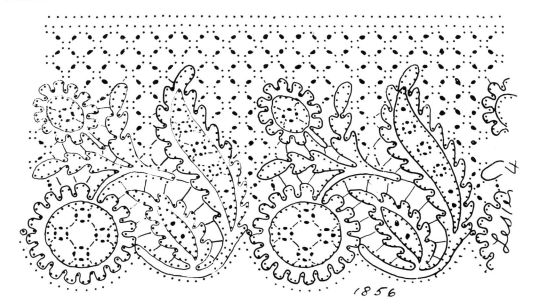

1856

82

Plate 5

Plate 6

Plate 9

Plate 12

Plate 13

Plate 14

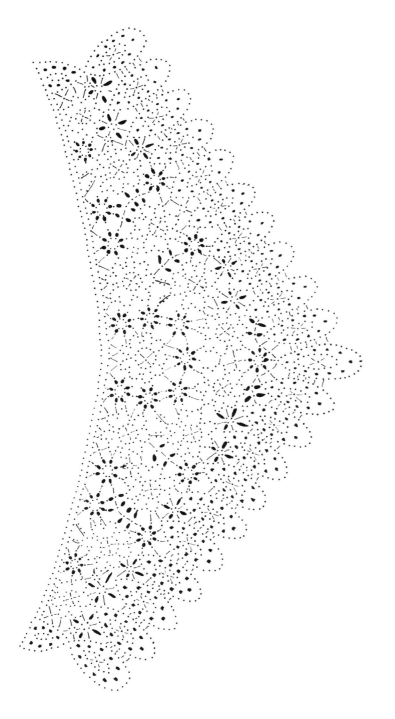

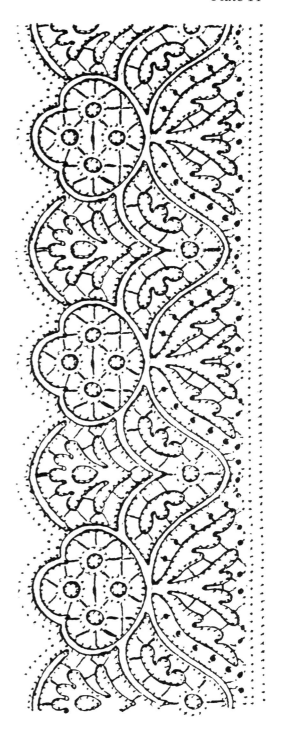

Plate 15

Plate 16

Plate 22

Plate 17

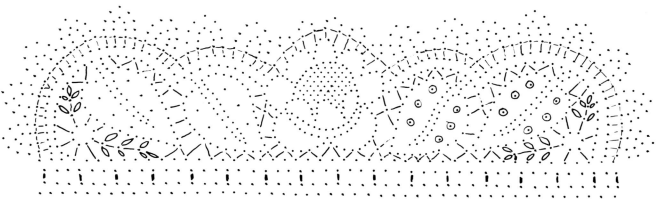

Plate 19

Plate 21

Plate 23

Plate 24

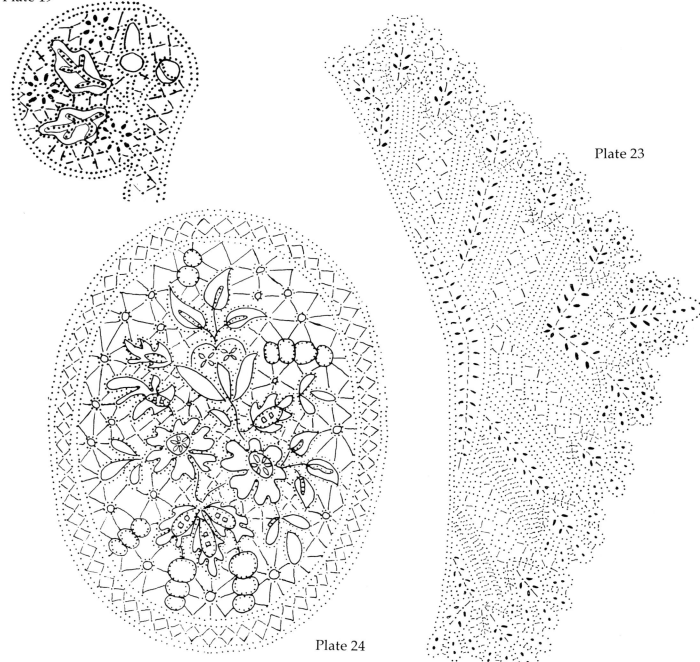

Plate 18

Plate 20

89

25

26

90

27

Adapted by the author from a draft inscribed 'Clarke' in the collection of Luton Museum.

28

Adapted by the author from a draft inscribed 'Sargent' in the collection of Luton Museum.

91

Other Lace, Costume and Embroidery Books

Bedfordshire Lace Patterns – A selection by Margaret Turner
0 903585 21 9   280 × 210mm, 112p, 145ill, folding sheet, limpbound

Manual of Bedfordshire Lace Pamela Robinson
0 903585 20 0   247 × 233mm, 112p, 151ill, limpbound

Lace Flowers and How to Make Them Joyce Willmot
0 903585 23 5   187 × 156mm, 76p, 46pl & diagr incl colour, hardbound

The Technique & Design of Cluny Lace L Paulis/Maria Rutgers
0 903585 18 9   220 × 174mm, 96p, 130ill, hardbound

Victorian Costume & Costume Accessories Anne Buck
0 903585 17 0   220 × 174mm, 224p, 90ill, paperback

Le Pompe 1559 Santina Levey/Pat Payne
(Patterns for Venetian Bobbin Lace)
0 903585 16 2   243 × 177mm, 128p, 97ill, paperback

Teach Yourself Torchon Lace Eunice Arnold
0 903585 08 1   240 × 190mm, 40p, 6workcards, 27ill, limpbound

Pillow Lace – A Practical Hand-book E Mincoff/M Marriage
0 903585 10 3   216 × 138mm, 304p, 2worksheets, 90ill, hardbound

Victorian Lace Patricia Wardle
0 903585 13 8   222 × 141mm, 304p, 82pl, hardbound

Thomas Lester His Lace & E Midlands Industry 1820–1905 Anne Buck
0 903585 09 X   280 × 210mm, 120p, 55pl, hardbound

The Romance of the Lace Pillow Thomas Wright
0 903585 12 X   222 × 141mm, 340p, 50pl, hardbound

Tailor's Pattern Book 1589 Juan de Alcega
(Libro de Geometria, Pratica y Traça)
0 903585 06 5   279 × 203mm, 244p, 137ill, clothbound

The Needlework of Mary Queen of Scots Margaret Swain
0 903585 22 7   280 × 212mm, 128p, 89pl incl 12 colour, paperback

Books on Textiles from:

RUTH BEAN Publishers
VICTORIA FARMHOUSE
CARLTON
BEDFORD MK43 7LP
ENGLAND